Celtic Christian Spirituality

Also by Oliver Davies and Fiona Bowie
and published by SPCK

The Rhineland Mystics 1989
Beguine Spirituality 1989
Hildegard of Bingen 1990
Meister Eckhart: Mystical Theologian 1991

Celtic
Christian Spirituality

AN ANTHOLOGY OF
MEDIEVAL AND MODERN SOURCES

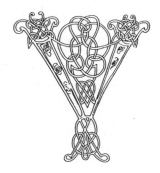

Edited by
OLIVER DAVIES *AND* FIONA BOWIE

Continuum New York

1995

The Continuum Publishing Company
370 Lexington Avenue
New York, NY 10017

Printed in Great Britain

Library of Congress Cataloging-in-Publication Data

Celtic Christian spirituality : an anthology of medieval and
modern sources / edited by Oliver Davies and Fiona Bowie.
p. cm.
Includes bibliographical references.
ISBN 0-8264-0835-4 (alk. paper)
1. Celtic Church.   2. Celts — Great Britain — Religion.
3. Celts — Ireland — Religion.   4. Spirituality — Great Britain —
History.   5. Spirituality — Ireland — History.   6. Great Britain —
Church history.   7. Ireland — Church history.   I. Davies,
Oliver.   II. Bowie, Fiona.
BR748.C35   1955
274'.0089'916 — dc20   95-8946 CIP

Cyflwynir y llyfr hwn i

Huw a Nancy, Meilyr ac Allison,
Catrin Haf ac Alun Gwynedd.

CONTENTS

ACKNOWLEDGEMENT

Our thanks go to Rachel Boulding, Brendan Walsh and Judith Long-
man, all of whom, in their capacity as editors, have waited patiently for
this book, and to the many friends and colleagues whose encourage-
ment and criticisms have been invaluable.

Oliver Davies and Fiona Bowie,
Lampeter

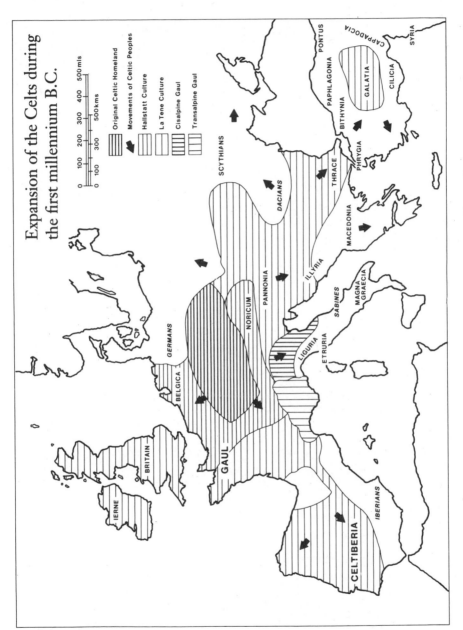

Expansion of the Celts during the first millennium B.C.

Legend:
- Original Celtic Homeland
- Movements of Celtic Peoples
- Hallstatt Culture
- La Tene Culture
- Cisalpine Gaul
- Transalpine Gaul

Scale: 0 100 200 300 400 500 mls / 0 100 300 500 kms

Labels on map:
IERNE, BRITAIN, GERMANS, BELGICA, GAUL, NORICUM, PANNONIA, ILLYRIA, SCYTHIANS, DACIANS, THRACE, MACEDONIA, PHRYGIA, BITHYNIA, PAPHLAGONIA, PONTUS, CAPPADOCIA, GALATIA, CILICIA, SYRIA, LIGURIA, SABINES, ETRURIA, MAGNA GRAECIA, CELTIBERIA, IBERIANS

Adapted from Peter Beresford Ellis, *The Celtic Empire*, Guild, London, 1990.

Introducing Celtic Christianity

Recent decades have witnessed an extraordinary revival of interest in the Celtic inheritance of Britain and Ireland.[1] The modern 'Celtic' prayers of David Adam (a priest from Lindisfarne), which draw inspiration from the collection of Gaelic religious literature known as the *Carmina Gadelica*, as well as the many anthologized editions of this work, have reached a wide and appreciative audience. An awareness of the Celtic past of these islands has been awakened in others by the medieval high crosses, often striking in both their execution and location, and rich in iconographic symbolism. The beauty, intricate detail and complexity of medieval gospel books such as the Book of Kells are a further tribute to the past genius of a Celtic Christian culture, hinting at values far removed from our modern consumerist society.

The revival of 'Celtic' arts, the development of neo-druidic groups and of 'Celtic Christian Churches' all testify to a desire to link the present to a past which is perceived as more ecological, imaginative, intuitive and theologically sound. For those who feel themselves to be modern Celts, particularly people who speak Celtic languages (Welsh, Irish and Scots Gaelic, Breton, and even Manx or Cornish), there is the added dimension of a search for roots, a sense of continuity and the validation of a separate and coherent identity, which is not merely the exotic 'other' of English or French culture.

There are numerous, often excellent, introductions to the Celtic world, pitched at different levels of interest and focusing on its various aspects (such as archaeology, mythology, literature). One may well ask, therefore, why yet another introduction to Celtic Christianity is thought necessary. But despite the growing number of publications in this field this book does, we believe, attempt something rather different. As with the other volumes in this series (*The Rhineland Mystics*, *Beguine Spirituality* and *Hildegard of Bingen*) our aim is to disseminate up-to-date scholarship to a non-specialist readership. In a field which abounds with popular representations and misrepresentations, feeding off a wide public interest in all things Celtic, it can become increasingly difficult to tell fact from fiction. We hope that the introductory essays will provide the reader with a map through this difficult terrain. In contrast to most other books on Celtic religion, the passages in this anthology cover a period of many centuries and come from many parts of the Celtic world. In moving from early medieval poetry and prose to nineteenth century oral literature and modern poetry we are seeking to demonstrate both the variety and the threads of continuity within the Celtic Christian world. The existence of 'Celtic Christianity' is, however, disputed by many reputable scholars. Understanding the complex web of desires, emotions and intuitions which lead some people to 're-discover' what others deny exists, will require some knowledge of the context of the study of Celtic history, and it is to this that we now turn.

The Search for Celtic Christianity

The retrieval of the Celtic Christian past is a process fraught with particular difficulties. In the first place, the very term 'Celtic' is essentially a recent invention. Although the Greeks and Romans used names such as *Keltoi, Galli* and *Celtae* to denote a wide range of different peoples, the term is first used in a more precise sense by linguists of the early eighteenth and nineteenth centuries who began to recognize a distinctive 'Celtic' family of languages.[2] Gradually, with an increase in knowledge, the term began to cover a diversity of artistic, social and cultural phenomena which appeared, to a greater or lesser degree, to be characteristic of the 'Celtic' peoples. The sense of a common Celtic identity among many in Ireland, Scotland, Wales, Brittany, Cornwall and the Isle of Man (and even Galicia), though real enough today, is decidedly a modern phenomenon, generated by economic and political factors which are far removed from the early and late medieval world. The monastic artists who produced the Book of Kells and carved the high crosses would not have thought of themselves as Celts.

The question at least needs to be asked therefore whether it is legitimate for us to talk of medieval 'Celtic' Christianity at all when the term 'Celtic' would itself have had no meaning in the Middle Ages. But in fact most of the ethnic terms habitually used by historians of early European history would not have been recognized, or would at least have been understood differently, by the peoples to whom they refer. While many of us may feel a European identity today, the Goths,

Lombards and Anglo-Saxons of the early Middle Ages emphatically did not. And yet these peoples will certainly feature in any study of 'European' history. The truth is that such broad ethnic categories constantly evolve and are useful to the historian precisely because they combine geographical and chronological meanings, as well as cultural and linguistic ones. In other words, they function well as tools with which to discuss and analyse the complex realities of human history precisely because they are inclusive and vague.

Great care must be taken with the term 'Celtic' however since all too often it is used in a way which suggests that nineteenth-century Scotland and pre-Christian Gaul, eighth-century Ireland and modern Brittany all somehow form a unified cultural unit: a single world populated by 'Celts'. In reality, of course, each period and each geographical area is distinct. The Celtic peoples, though related by language and aspects of culture, have all experienced different histories, and have had to negotiate their own identity with respect to dominant powers in diverse ways. Their spiritualities are also varied and we should beware of extracting specific elements that catch our eye from periods which are as far apart as, for instance, modern Italy and ancient Rome and presenting these together as if they all constituted a single and timeless phenomenon called 'Celtic spirituality'. In almost two thousand years of Celtic Christian history, we should expect to see more divergence and difference than continuity.

The view that the Celts had their own distinctive Church is one of the chief ways in which Celtic Christianity has been misread. We live in a Christian world governed by denominations, and it is natural that we should project this into the past. In truth however the Western Church was united as one Church until the Reformation, and what might be construed as a conflict between the 'Celtic Church' and the 'Roman Catholic Church' was in fact competition between different trends and traditions within a single and still united Church. A number of prominent historians have refuted the idea of the existence in any way of 'a Celtic Church' as a distinct institutional body, pointing also to the differences in church organization among the different Celtic peoples.[3] In attempting to come to an authentic understanding of medieval Celtic Christianity, our legitimate desire to find an alternative Christian model for today must be matched by a close and informed reading of historical sources.

It was in fact inter-denominational rivalry which formed the context for the earliest systematic explorations into the field of Celtic Christianity. Both English and Welsh Reformers believed that they had discovered in the Ancient British (i.e. Celtic) Church of old a body which was both ancient and episcopal and evidently not to be identified with the Roman Catholic Church of the Counter-Reformation.[4] Indeed, this remained the paramount point of interest with regard to Celtic Christianity for several centuries, and the desire to discover an ancient alternative to Roman Catholicism is still a factor in the minds even of some modern commentators, who like to point, with some justification, to its affinities with the Orthodox East.

Despite the ambiguity over the term 'Celtic' and the lack of any consensus as to what it actually designates, we feel justified in using the term 'Celtic Christianity' for two reasons. First, because there undoubtedly are some distinctive and important Christian emphases which thread their way through the religious imagination of Celtic-speaking peoples, and second, though just as important, many Christians living in Celtic countries today choose to regard themselves as Celts. Such an identity is to some extent, like all ethnicities, based on a mythologized reading of the past, but it has its own reality and exigencies, and should not be dismissed too lightly.

The Origins of the Celts

Peoples speaking Celtic languages once covered much of Europe. The earliest traces of Celtic-language groups date from the late Urnfield culture of the first millennium BC, although the first visible expression of a grouping which has been unequivocally identified as Celtic on linguistic grounds is the Hallstatt culture, which developed in what is modern Austria in 700–500 BC.[5] It was the war-like, iron-using people of the late Hallstatt period, together with the La Tène culture which evolved from it, with which the classical civilizations of Greece and Rome came into immediate contact and who are remembered in their literature as wild, scantily clad warriors. The fine and distinctive metalwork of La Tène is the surviving expression of a widespread and sophisticated culture which straddled Europe in the period from around 500 BC to the time of the subjugation of the continental Celtic peoples by Julius Caesar in the first century BC. Celtic remains have been found as far afield as southern Italy, Portugal and Spain, Denmark and modern Turkey (the home of the Galatians who may have spoken a Celtic language when St Paul wrote to them in around 54 AD). Roman conquest, and then migration by Germanic tribes into central and southern Europe, brought to an end the high period of continental Celtic civilization which we can glimpse today only in the more spectacular archaeological finds of deposits in river, shaft and lake, and by the remarks of their classical contemporaries, curious as to the nature and customs of the peoples they were set to conquer.

Ancient Celtic society, at least as we see it through the eyes of contemporary Greek and Roman writers, was one which had the values of the earliest heroic age of Greece and Rome.[6] This means to say that it was a warrior culture in which the greatest value was placed upon achievement in war and upon the qualities of self-denying strength and fearless valour by which it was achieved. But the power of the warrior was balanced in Celtic society by other no less important elements. There are signs of great ingenuity and dexterity in the design and manufacture of tools, such as ploughs and spoked wheels, as well as in the magnificent torques and brooches which have been discovered all over Europe. Indeed, the inventiveness of the Celt is apparent not only in high art but also in the more popular and widespread forms of decoration and craftsmanship that are typical even of everyday objects. The Celtic designer delighted in riddles and ambiguity, in rhythm and fluidity of form, and in abstract harmonies at the expense of the naturalism and idealism of the Greeks. But Celtic art also showed its vigour in the ability of the craftsmen to absorb and transform foreign influences at different stages of history, whether from Greece or Rome, Etruria or Scythia, while maintaining a distinctively Celtic continuity of form and style.

Pre-Christian Celtic Religion

Early Celtic societies, with their characteristic division into king, druidic class, bardic class, law-givers and artisans, seem also to have found their common focus in religion. Celts, as the Romans observed, were very religious people.[7] There was no aspect of life which was not in some way touched by the intricate webs of ritual and belief that gave life and meaning to the Celtic world. Time and seasons were calculated according to religious criteria, with the druids pronouncing upon the most auspicious moment for undertakings. Divination was commonplace, including perhaps divination by human sacrifice, as was the reading of auguries within the natural world, especially involving the behaviour of birds. Religion demanded sacrifice, particularly in times of war when victory was paid for by dedicating the spoils of victory to the relevant god. Indeed, much Celtic wealth seems to have found its way for cultic reasons into the earth, rivers or lakes to be swiftly retrieved by Roman soldiers or, centuries later, by the painstaking work of archaeologists.

Indeed, there are notable differences between the religiosity of the Celts and that of the Romans, who were methodically destroying continental Celtic civilization during the first century BC. In the first place, we find among the Celts an absence of the written word, which contrasts with the philosophically sophisticated religious writings of the Mediterranean world. Celtic society had clearly not begun to emulate the standards of literacy of Greece and Rome, and shows all the signs of having been vigorously oral. Power was invested in the druidic class, who protected traditional knowledge ranging from cosmology to genealogy and law, by an oral system of learning which was based, as such systems are, on simple and repetitive poetic forms in order to facilitate the task of memory. Although traditional knowledge among the Celts may have been — and probably was — very sophisticated, its oral character suggests its decidedly unphilosophical (in the modern sense) nature, and its indebtedness to poetry, mythology and imagery.

Second, there is a tribal dimension. Caesar mentions the fact that a Celt who was banned by his or her own community from partaking in the sacrifices suffered total social isolation. It would be difficult to parallel this in the contemporary classical world, but similarly closed social communities can be found among some of the technologically less developed societies that exist today.

Third, Celtic religion appeared to be a markedly local phenomenon. The cult of a particular deity was generally linked to a specific location, whether this was a river or lake or one of the dark forest groves that so shocked the Romans. The gods of the classical peoples, on the other hand, were more mobile and their temples might appear anywhere within the Empire. We see among the Celts an interpenetration of religion and landscape in a way that surpasses anything we might find in the late classical world. This is an important point. It means that, for the Celt, God, or the transcendent, did not speak to the human community outside and beyond its natural environment. Rather, God spoke to humanity precisely *within* the natural world. In other words, nature, the cosmos, was taken up into and formed part of the dialogue between human beings and God. This is in stark contrast to the tendency we find in the late classical world to abstract human community from its environment and to confine religious dialogue to the realm of the spirit. We might note here however that there are certain parallels between this Celtic approach and the religious consciousness of the Hebrews with their promised land.

The attempt to recreate early Celtic religion is precarious and is based upon the evidence of archaeology, historical linguistics and place-names, combined with anecdotes and snippets of information recorded by some of the writers of antiquity. To this must be added perspectives that can be discerned in the earliest Irish and Welsh writings which, although they date from a later period, are likely in some degree to reflect the beliefs and practices of earlier centuries. We can imagine that early Celtic religion offered society a means of manipulating the powerful spirit forces that were everywhere present in their world. It is likely that the early Celt lived in a domain that was filled with unseen presences, including possibly those of potentially hostile ancestor spirits whose skulls may have been carefully tended by their living relatives, as they are in many sub-Saharan African and other societies today.[8] There may also have been particular individuals who, dressed in skins, entered trance-like states in which they believed that they were carried on a spirit journey into the bodies of animals in order to effect an act of healing, like the shamans of the Arctic north or of South America.[9] We can imagine too that the topography of the tribal area would have been filled with religious resonances, particular places (such as springs and lakes) being passage-ways to the unseen world where humans could contact, supplicate or control the hidden forces that seemed to determine the health and prosperity of individuals and the community.

Although we can point to many continental Celtic representations of the horned god Cernunos (who may after all simply be a shamanic figure dressed as a stag), to early Irish inspirational bards who may have dressed in bird feathers, and to goddess-like muses such as the Welsh Ceridwen or Ogyrfen who were the source of bardic inspiration and song, we can be neither specific nor certain on any of these matters.[10] It is surely the case however that by looking at the full range of contemporary human societies, we can glimpse at least the possibilities of what early Celtic religion may have been.

The Roots of Celtic Christianity

An account of the history of Christianity among the Celtic-speaking peoples must consider the forms of religious and spiritual life that predominated at that time. Prior to the arrival of Christianity the Celtic peoples had a dynamic and vital indigenous religion. The religious outlook, sensibilities and practices of British, and later Irish, converts would not have changed overnight, but would have fused in various ways with the new faith. Insular Christianity (that is, Christianity in Britain and Ireland) therefore took on a distinctively 'Celtic' colour, and it is this which interests so many observers today.[11]

The Celtic inhabitants of Britain and Ireland during this period were divided into two main groups who spoke distinct but related languages. In what is now England, Wales and southern Scotland there lived Brythonic Celts, who spoke the 'Brythonic' or 'British' language (related to Welsh and Cornish, from which Breton is also derived). Although divided into numerous, often warring, tribes the Brythonic Celts also maintained close links with one another, intermarried and spoke mutually comprehensible dialects. In Ireland, western Scotland and the Isle of Man were the Goedelic Celts (who spoke languages which evolved into Irish, Scots Gaelic and Manx). These two branches of the Celtic-speaking family never lost contact with one another. Many individuals (like St Patrick in the fifth century AD) moved easily between the two cultural areas which were linked by sea routes. Extensive Irish settlements have been found in Wales, particularly on the coasts, and the existence of common place-names and church dedications confirm the narrative evidence of continued contact between Britain and Ireland.

The experience of Roman occupation in what is now known as England, southern Scotland and much of Wales did, however, mean that the Brythonic and Goedelic Celts followed different historical paths. It is usual to regard early Ireland as the model for insular Celtic civilization since of all the Celtic societies of north western Europe, Ireland alone represents a Celtic tradition which was virtually untouched by *latinitas* and *romanitas*, which is to say the culture and civilization of the Roman Empire. The Irish were never conquered by the Roman armies that put an end to continental Celtic civilization. But it is in fact to mainland Britain that we must look for the earliest signs of Celtic Christianity, precisely because the Brythonic Celts, the forerunners of the modern Welsh, Cornish and southern Scots, suffered defeat at the hands of Caesar's troops and remained for several centuries an integral part of the late Roman world.

BRITAIN

The new faith came to the British Isles through the Roman forces and administrators, and from the numerous traders and other wanderers who traversed the Roman domains. The first signs of a Christian presence in Britain date from some two hundred years after the death of Jesus. The martyrdoms of Aaron and Julius, probably in Caerleon in Gwent (south east Wales), and Alban can be dated to the middle of the third century,[12] and British bishops were present at the Council of Arles in 314. Two archaeological finds from this period suggest a relatively peaceful coexistence of the new religion with some of the symbols and practices of the older pagan way of life. The hoard of silver church plate which dates from around 350 AD, found in 1975 at Water Newton near Peterborough, includes Christian votive tablets, while the Hinton St Mary mosaic seems to combine an image of Christ detailed upon the floor with pagan religious motifs.[13]

Very little is known about the character and quality of the Christian life in Britain in this early period, but the scant evidence we have points to the existence of a strongly Romanized Church, most prevalent among the Romano-British elite, the wealthy and entrepreneurial Brythonic Celts who were the people most directly in contact with the occupiers. It was a Church whose language was overwhelmingly Latin and whose diocesan structure, based upon local centres of population, reflected the Roman pattern of civil organization. The three British bishops who attended the Council of Arles came from London, York and either Lincoln or Colchester. Romano-British Christians suffered with the rest of Christendom during the persecutions of the mid-third century and rejoiced when in 313 the Edict of Milan marked a new period of liberation and security for the Christian Church.

Although the remoteness of the Romano-British Church from the continental sources of ecclesiastical power needs to be stressed (it was little more than an off-shore appendage to the Church in Gaul), it did at least produce a theology which caused a considerable stir in the great centres of the Christian world. Pelagius, who was probably a Brythonic Celt by birth, lent his name to the heresy which appears to have arisen in monastic circles and which was particularly influential in Britain and southern Gaul. Prosper of Aquitaine tells us that Pope Celestine was prompted to send Germanus, Bishop of Auxerre, on a mission to Britain in 429 in order to counter the Pelagians, which he did successfully, though only temporarily.

It is not easy to reconstruct Pelagianism in detail today, since many of the relevant texts are lost and much of what survives is Catholic polemic, but the movement characteristically stressed the role of the human will in the process of redemption. Pelagius himself believed that God-given human nature was itself capable of distinguishing the good from the bad, thus of initiating the movement of the individual towards God. In theological terms this was to emphasize nature at the expense of grace, or at least to confine the operation of grace to an external sphere, denying that it acted also within the human will. This view evoked an emphatic response from the great Augustine, Bishop of Hippo, who developed his own theory of grace in his many anti-Pelagian writings. Pelagianism, in the form it took among the most eager supporters of Pelagius' position, was repeatedly condemned by church councils, not least for denying the concept of original sin and opposing the baptism of infants. We can postulate that such a positive view of human nature may itself have been a reflection of a greater optimism towards the created world in early Celtic culture than was the case in that of the Mediterranean and North Africa, although, without knowing more about Pelagius' relation to native culture, such a hypothesis must remain speculative.[14] The themes of nature, freedom and grace became a perennial concern, of course, and were to reappear forcefully during the Reformation when, ironically, it could be said that the Protestants generally adopted a quasi-Augustinian position and the Catholics a quasi-Pelagian one.

The Romano-British Church survived until the first half of the fifth century when, after the withdrawal of the Roman forces in 409, the Romanized, Celtic areas of Britain came under increasing pressure from the vigorous assaults of the Irish from the west, the Picts from the north and, most importantly, from the early English peoples who were seizing land from the east. Over a period of time the territory of the Romano-British Church sharply contracted in the face of such pagan advances. The Brythonic lands, largely to the west of the country, which offered the invaders most resistance did so on account of the generally remote and inaccessible character of their terrain, which had served also to restrict the degree of Roman influence in these parts. The Romano-British Church therefore, which sent no more bishops to continental councils, was cut off from the continental well-springs of the Christian religion and increasingly took on the aspect of an insular and archaic foundation. It was not necessarily the case that Christianity was completely extinguished in the eastern, English parts of Britain (nor that the indigenous Brythonic-speaking inhabitants of these parts actually moved west), but evidence for its survival there, prior to the evangelization of the English in the seventh century, is meagre.[15]

With the collapse of the Romano-British Church in the fifth century, Christianity was restricted to Strathclyde and Cumbria in the north, through Wales and the borders to Devon and Cornwall in the south. In addition, there increasingly occurred the movement of peoples from the south west of Britain to Armorica or Brittany in north west France. But despite the presence of figures such as St Ninian at Whithorn in the north, it is to the Welsh church that we must turn for the most numerous British sources in the early period, since we possess almost no literary sources for Christian life in Brythonic Scotland, Cornwall and Brittany until the later Middle Ages.[16] Indeed, the early Welsh were keen to stress their historical links with the old Roman civilization and with the religion that it had introduced, and it is worth noting that the very term 'Welsh' is an early English word which means 'Romanized Celt'.[17] There is much evidence to support continuity moreover, since there are almost no accounts of conversion in the earliest Welsh literature, the Welsh/British Church that Gildas berates in the early sixth century is apparently already hopelessly corrupt, and there is evidence for at least one sixth-century territorial diocese (along the lines of the Romano-British Church) in either Welsh Bicknor or near Kenderchurch in south east Wales.[18]

The spiritual inspiration for the early Welsh Church seems to have come in the main from the monks of the Middle East and their counterparts in southern Gaul. The *Lives* of the early Welsh saints are full of references and allusions to the monasticism of the desert; the Eastern monastic ascetic ideal, particularly as this was mediated by the works of Cassian, evidently provided a powerful role model in Wales, as it did in other Celtic lands.[19] It is likely that during the fifth and sixth centuries individuals inspired by these ideals sought solitude and a life of work and prayer, attracting to themselves like-minded followers who established communities about them, as had been the pattern in fourth-century Egypt. In course of time, some such communities developed into small townships while other sites retained their original ascetical and eremetical character. There is some evidence to suggest that the communities of the far west (such as Bardsey to the north, Caldy and St David's in the south west), which were closer to Ireland, may have reflected a more ascetical lifestyle, while those of the east (such as Llantwit Major), which were closer to England, may have laid greater stress upon learning.[20]

Perhaps the most important single feature about the Welsh Church during the early Middle Ages is its remoteness from the urban centres of ecclesiastical power and hence its tendency to retain customs that elsewhere were rapidly overtaken by the harmonization process that was characteristic of the Christian Church throughout Europe at this time. The belated acceptance by the Celtic churches of the Roman method of calculating the date of Easter at the Synod of Whitby in 664 is but one example of this. The Welsh medieval Church reflects earlier ways therefore, and is not neatly organized into monks, clergy and laity. Rather the *clasau*, or religious communities, were probably based on a proliferation of local rules, variously adhered to. 'Monasticism' was widespread, if not the norm, even if it was only a small minority that were celibate, committed to a rigorous lifestyle and, perhaps, living in solitude like the 'saints of old'.

It was in this environment, however, that something of the distinctive Christianity, which resulted from the fusion of the old religion with the new, could survive. And in fact there is much that is original in a body of literature which occurs in a thirteenth-century manuscript, based on earlier sources, known as the *Black Book of Carmarthen*. First, we find in these works an unusually positive attitude to the creation and, second, they constitute in themselves a phenomenon which cannot be paralleled outside the Celtic world. It was the convention during the Middle Ages for monks to communicate with other monks in Latin prose, for this was the appropriate medium of the Church. The fact that these works from the *Black Book of Carmarthen*, which date from the ninth or tenth centuries, were poems and were written in Welsh, although they were composed by monks and are often expressly concerned with monastic life, is itself an indication of how different the Welsh religious tradition could be (pages 28–31). Specifically, it shows the central place that poetry enjoyed in medieval Welsh Christianity. In fact one poem from this corpus lists the devotional practices that are required of a pious soul and includes 'listening to the songs of clear-speaking poets'.[21] The poetic tradition, then, was one of the principal ways in which a distinctive spiritual sensibility was maintained in Wales, a fact which is less surprising when we remember that the earliest Christian poetic tradition must have emerged from the bardism which was central to the religion of the pre-Christian Celtic world.

The 'archaic' period in Wales came to an end with the arrival of the Normans, who brought with them many of the norms of continental Christianity. For the first time the major religious Orders of the Catholic Church, principally the Cistercians, took root in Wales. The ancient Celtic foundations either gave way to the new Orders or themselves conformed, frequently by adopting the Augustinian Rule and becoming Canons. It would be wrong to view this time as marking the end of the existence of a 'Celtic Church' in Wales (and Ireland), however, since the Church in the Celtic countries never constituted a separate entity but rather a geographical and cultural area in which the rationalization and reorganization of the Catholic Church were slow to arrive. The new integration into European ways brought change, but also quickened a Welsh national consciousness and represented a welcome expansion of Welsh cultural horizons. Nor did it necessarily prove entirely inimical to the indigenous religion, since a number of the Welsh Cistercian houses became bastions of Welsh culture and tradition. A Franciscan such as Madog ap Gwallter, and the anonymous Dominican author of *Food for the Soul* still reflect a deeply Celtic sensibility in their work despite the European character of their religious formation.

IRELAND

If the earliest origins of Celtic Christianity are to be found on mainland Britain, then its flowering was in Ireland. But the coming of Christianity to Ireland was markedly different from that of most of Europe in that Christianity was not a religion fostered or even approved by the state, since Ireland lay outside the confines of the Roman Empire. There is only scant and contradictory evidence for the earliest period of evangelization. Prosper of Aquitaine stated in his chronicle for the year 431 that 'Palladius was ordained by Pope Celestine and sent to the Irish believers in Christ as their first bishop'.[22] This has been taken to indicate the existence of a sizeable Christian community in Ireland prior to the missionary activity of Patrick, and indeed, it is entirely reasonable that just such a community existed, evolving through contact with the Celtic Christians of western Britain. It is notable that the foundations that are linked with the name of Palladius by tradition are all in Leinster, in the eastern part of Ireland, and thus a short sea journey away from the north western coast of Wales.

The most important documents for the life and work of Patrick are those by his own hand, the *Declaration* and the *Letter to Coroticus*, although these offer us only an uncertain picture of his provenance and background. It seems likely however that he was from a Christian family and came from western Britain (perhaps around Carlisle), from where he was snatched by an Irish raiding party and taken into slavery. He then escaped and made his way back to Britain, but returned later to Ireland with a deep commitment to work as a missionary there. It is likely that he carried out his ministry mainly in the north of Ireland, among the Ulaid, around the middle of the fifth century. Muirchú's *Life of Patrick* was written in Ireland in the seventh century and marks an upsurge of interest in the figure of Patrick after some two hundred years of silence. This trend culminates in the *Book of Armagh*, written in the north of Ireland in 807, which juxtaposes the writings of Patrick with Muirchú's *Life* and the prestigious *Life of St Martin of Tours*, in order to reinforce the claim of Armagh to the Primacy of all Ireland.

Although Patrick and Palladius were both bishops, and therefore represented the conventional diocesan structure of the Church of Gaul and elsewhere, the early evangelization of Ireland was largely marked by the spread of monasticism. From the beginning of the sixth century onwards we find an abundance of monastic foundations which are linked with individual saints such as Buithe (Monasterboice), Brigid (Kildare), Finnian (Clonard), Ciarán (Clonmacnois), Colum mac Crimthainn (Terryglass) and Brendan (Clonfert). The immediate origins of this monastic movement remain obscure, although the monastic and ascetical ideals which originated in Egypt in the fourth century may have come to Ireland from Gaul and Wales in the fifth. One reason that has been put forward for the rapid spread of monasticism in Ireland is that the monasteries were taken over into the kinship pattern of the ruling families. Certainly foundations often remained within the possession of a single family, and different monasteries within the same confederations were linked by the ties of kinship, as well as by more spiritual bonds. Early Irish society was deeply tribal in its structure, and it is very likely this that both prepared the ground for the ideal of spiritual community that came with the advent of monasticism, and influenced its form. It is certainly the case that we can observe in early Ireland diocesan structures which are based either upon the bishop, or upon the abbot or upon individuals who fulfill the office of both.

Among the many figures of early Irish monasticism, two in particular stand out. The first is Colum Cille (also known as Columba, 521/22–597), whose *Life* was written by his relative Adomnán some one hundred years after his death. Colum Cille was linked with the powerful Uí Néill tribe of northern Ireland and with the royal dynasty of Leinster. He founded monasteries in Derry and Durrow and, in 563, left Ireland to found a community off the Scottish coast at Iona. The island of Iona was still in the sphere of influence of the Picts at this point, although in course of time Irish language and culture would come to dominate the whole of the western part of Scotland. Iona itself became a greatly influential centre of Irish Christianity from where the religion of the Irish passed to Northumbria, where it took root at Lindisfarne and elsewhere, and even extended down into parts of East Anglia. The happy coalescence of Irish and early English culture and Christianity during this period, which led to what is termed the 'Insular' tradition, suffered a blow with the Synod of Whitby in 664 and controversy over the calculation of Easter. Nevertheless, even after this time, there was still much travel and interchange, with Irishmen holding senior posts in the English Church, Englishmen studying in Ireland or at Irish foundations, and visible co-operation in the fields of learning and art.[23]

The second leading figure of this period was Columbanus (543–615), who was born in Leinster, trained in Bangor (County Down) and left Ireland in 587 for Gaul. In contrast to Colum Cille, we have a good number of works from the pen of Columbanus which convey the picture of a passionate and able Christian leader. The works of Columbanus include a *Rule* and a *Penitential* (for monks and laity) and several impressive sermons and letters (pages 74–77). Columbanus was a principal mediator of Irish Christianity to the Continent and was the founder of important monasteries such as Luxeuil in south east France and Bobbio in northern Italy. The life-long and voluntary commitment of Columbanus to exile from his homeland is an outstanding example of *peregrinatio pro Christo*, or 'wandering for the sake of Christ', whereby a monk would cut himself off from his own extended family as an act of ascetical discipline. It is these wandering Irish monks in exile who were responsible for bringing Christianity to large areas of central Europe, as well as introducing to many other parts the advantages of Irish Christianity with its discipline, commitment and devotion to learning and the arts.

The religious vocation of these early monks was an ideal which was to reappear time and again in the history of the Irish Church. Its first and major resurgence occurred in the eighth century with the emergence of a movement known as the *Célí Dé*, or 'servants/friends of God'. The reform spread out from Munster in southern Ireland to other parts of the country and even beyond, to the western seaboard of Britain. It found its centre however in the Dublin area where leaders such as Maelrúain of Tallaght and Dublittir of Finglas inspired their followers with a love of renunciation and radical monasticism. The movement is associated also with the flowering of Irish religious poetry, especially the hermit poetry, and with the Stowe Missal, which is one of our chief sources for the early Irish liturgical tradition.

The Irish Church was badly disrupted from the ninth century onwards by Viking attacks, as was the case elsewhere in Europe, but it was the advent of the English and the Normans in the twelfth century which, as we have seen with Wales, led to the greater integration of Ireland into the forms and ways of continental Christianity.

THE MODERN PERIOD

Both the Reformation and the Catholic Counter-Reformation proved inimical to much that was distinctive in early Celtic Christianity. In addition, literacy and more developed technology, mobility of populations and of ideas lessened the remoteness and isolation of the Celtic countries. And yet important social, geographical and cultural forces have combined to ensure a far greater degree of continuity for the Celtic peoples than has been the case for their major European neighbours. In the first place, social change has come more slowly in the remote western parts of Scotland, Ireland, Brittany and Wales. It is here that the Celtic languages have been preserved, ensuring the survival of a vigorous oral culture for much of the modern period. Oral and geographically isolated cultures can be peculiarly shielded from the more radical change engendered by books and the written word within an urban environment, especially if — as has increasingly been the case in recent centuries — the very identity of a people is bound up with an oral, Celtic-language culture surviving in precarious opposition to the cultural innovation of the English or French-speaking world. In such a cultural milieu, moreover, especially when the English (or French) world is outrightly hostile to the survival of the oral medium, the forces of cultural conservatism can become far greater than in secure urban centres of cultural power. In that case there is a tendency for the bearers of the oral tradition precisely to anchor themselves in the past, as a form of self-definition, and as a secure point of orientation in a generally hostile cultural landscape.

It is legitimate to speak of the survival of a Celtic Christian tradition in the modern period therefore, but it is to the oral traditions that we must turn, generally those of poetry and song. In the case of Wales there are surprising parallels between the early monks, with their sense of community and emphasis upon religious poetry, and the culture of popular Methodism in the eighteenth century and later, when the chapels became the focus for a strongly communal spirituality which found its prime expression in powerful hymns such as those of Williams Pantycelyn (1717–1791) and Ann Griffiths (1776–1805). A Calvinist Methodist poet such as Thomas Jones (1756–1820) still stands within an identifiable poetic tradition going back to the Middle Ages. But it is the religious songs of the Highlands and Western Isles of Scotland, which were gathered by Alexander Carmichael (1832–1912) during the second half of the nineteenth century and published initially in two volumes in 1900 as the *Carmina Gadelica*, which are perhaps the finest example of the survival of a distinctively Celtic religious spirit in the modern world.

Alexander Carmichael, a Gaelic speaker from the Island of Lismore near Oban in Scotland, worked for the Customs and Excise Department, which gave him an extensive familiarity with the western Highlands and Islands of the Outer and Inner Hebrides where, between 1855 and 1899, he collected an enormous amount of oral Gaelic material. After Carmichael's death, a further three volumes of the *Carmina Gadelica* were published at intervals, all of which were based upon Carmichael's original notes.[24] In order to evaluate his achievement it is important to remember the social and historical context in which Carmichael worked. He lived at a time when the status of Gaelic culture was particularly low and he belonged to a literary and national movement which was keen both to protect the interests of Gaelic culture and to establish its credentials. If the items in the *Ortha na Gaidheal/Carmina Gadelica* sometimes seem more literary and polished than might be expected in oral material of this kind, then this probably reflects the editor's extensive editing due to his understandable desire that the material be accorded its own dignity.

The situation in Ireland with respect to Irish language culture showed certain parallels. Douglas Hyde (1860–1949), born into an Anglican family in County Roscommon, was founder and President of the Gaelic League; he served also as the first President of an independent Ireland (1938–45). A man of extensive interests and talents, Hyde published plays, poetry (historical and literary), as well as academic works. He is, however, perhaps best remembered for the bilingual collection of songs and stories, originally printed in various journals, which comprise *The Songs of Connacht*. These included love songs, drinking songs, songs in praise of women, various tales and religious material. *The Religious Songs of Connacht*, from which the selections in this volume are taken, was first published in book form in 1906. Like Carmichael, Hyde was an admirer of the Gaelic-speaking peasantry, and recognized the wealth of oral literature which was commonly disregarded by the educated, and in danger of disappearing along with the Irish language itself.

One marked difference between the Irish and Scottish situation was that many more Irish texts were recorded in manuscript, and so the line of demarcation between a purely oral and a written culture in Ireland is not always easily drawn. Some poems by the thirteenth-century bard Donagha More O'Daly, for instance, were still learnt and recited orally by people in the nineteenth century. As Hyde comments, 'They were as well known in the province of Munster as they were in Connacht, and some of them are in the mouths of the people to this very day.' In terms of content, there are both similarities and differences between the *Carmina Gadelica* and the *Religious Songs of Connacht*. Both include charms, prayers for protection against the evil eye or fairies, herbal cures, curses, tales concerning Irish mythological characters such as Ossian and Fionn, and saints, and both contain a number of the same traditional Catholic prayers. But the *Religious Songs of Connacht* also contains a large body of literature concerning priests, a genre absent from the *Carmina Gadelica*. There is also far more sentimental Catholic piety in the Irish material, and long moralistic tales which, if known in Scotland, Carmichael either failed or chose not to record.

The final section of this volume is an anthology of modern poetry from the Celtic countries, which is set in context with an introductory essay. For many, it is in poems that something vital remains of an ancient tradition, and poets, more than most, often have reason to explore the roots of the tradition of which they themselves are a part. The Celtic cultures remain surprisingly responsive to the work of poets, who enjoy a popularity and a fame that living English or French poets can only envy. Their work can thus become a point of transmission to a community of an earlier way of seeing the world, revitalized and transformed by the personal art and creativity of the individual poet.

Celtic Christianity Today

There is a widespread interest throughout the Western world in the spirituality of indigenous peoples, from Native Americans to the highland culture of the Philippines. But a personal engagement with such religious systems leads to precisely the same problem facing those who are attracted to the spirituality of the Celtic peoples. How can we share in something we much admire when we ourselves are not part of that particular culture which is the very foundation of the spirituality? How can one participate in a 'Celtic Christianity' if one is living in New York or London, and therefore unable to engage with the particular spirituality of place which is so characteristic a part of the Celtic tradition? For the majority of people who actually live through the medium of a Celtic language the great Celtic Christian civilizations of the Middle Ages, even if ever present in place and personal names, are far removed from the daily concerns of finding work, coping with unemployment, dealing with English- (or French-)speaking inward migration, and the continual struggle to preserve a language and community life in the face of sometimes seemingly overwhelming odds. And yet, even if an authentic Celtic Christian culture is in a certain sense exclusive, and to a large degree a thing of the past, there are still all kinds of ways in which we may learn from this inheritance and make its wisdom our own.

The first thing we can learn from Celtic Christianity concerns its physicality. Many early monks were inspired by the monastic and ascetical ideals of the Egyptian desert and sought to re-enact the achievements of Anthony and his followers on the islands and mountains of their homeland. Many took themselves into exile, 'crucifying their body on the blue waves', like Columba. But perhaps the chief expression of this spirit was the penitential tradition, which laid great stress upon the voluntary acceptance of physical discomfort and deprivation as a way to God. Although penance is altogether out of favour today, the typically Celtic emphasis upon it has something important to teach us. In the first place, it reminds us that we are embodied beings. There is much within traditional Christianity, particularly in some of its Protestant forms, which seems to stress the reception of the gospel in the mind to the exclusion of the body. Yet neither is early Celtic penitential discipline to be identified with the refinements of self-mortification that we associate with Post-Tridentine Catholicism. It is not so much the unwholesome desire to punish oneself or one's body

for today

that we encounter in early Celtic penitential texts (although this certainly also exists) but rather a sense of spiritual opportunity – that glory is the reward of 'long penance, daily' (page 53). Penance then is a way of including the body in our dialogue with God. The dynamic here is different from our own. We generally have little sense of the need for penance today, and equally little sense of the reality of glory.

physicality

Linked perhaps with the stress upon physicality, there is a persistent emphasis in the Celtic texts upon the place of nature within the Christian revelation. We see this in a number of saints' *Lives*, where creatures spontaneously offer their services to the Christian saint, or seek refuge with him or her (page 65); but it is no less evident in early Irish and Welsh poems which may well have been written by monks. There the natural world is the context in which the poet delights and for which and with which he offers praise (page 28). It is certainly this acknowledgement and affirmation of nature which is one of the most distinctive aspects of Celtic Christianity. In the classical model, by way of contrast, the natural world, if it is mentioned at all, is in nearly every instance that which the Christian saint merely *controls*. The Celtic Christian recognition of the place of nature, and refusal to set up sharp oppositions between the worlds of grace and humanity and the natural realm, is undoubtedly of great importance to those who seek to restore a more positive and responsible relation between human beings and the environment in our own day.

place of nature –

Furthermore, we find in Celtic Christianity a valuing of the creative imagination of the individual, evident in a particular way in the High Crosses, in the tradition of illumination which culminates in the Book of Kells and in the Christian bardic tradition. Of course, other cultures have produced religious art of the highest quality, but the place of the scribe within early Irish society and the belief of Welsh poets that the Holy Spirit was their direct inspiration remind us that the creative arts stood not at the margins of the Church but at its very centre.

creative arts at its centre

Finally, Celtic Christianity is filled with the spirit of community, whether in terms of monasticism or the close-knit rural societies of the post-medieval world. The bards too had a public function and spoke directly to a community, as many poets still do. And from a theological point of view the Trinity, which is the ultimate ground and model of community, held a special place in Celtic religious life, being the primary way in which most Celtic thinkers and artists understood the Godhead. Although the sense of community of the early Celts was rooted primarily in the extended family and tribe, there are hints also of

community

a more universalist understanding, mediated through the Church and contained in particular in reflections upon the origins of the human body. We can read texts such as the *Creation of Adam* and *The Evernew Tongue* (pages 79–81) as conveying an understanding of the human person as being essentially in community with the natural world, with the whole of humanity and with the body of the resurrected Christ. Community is of vital concern for us too, on both a local and a universal level, since Western society has so often been caught between rampant individualism on the one hand and aggressive nationalism on the other.

In sum therefore, the distinctive tenor of Celtic Christianity is one of a life-affirming integration which finds its theological centre in the vision of God as divine creativity and community, which is the Christian doctrine of the Trinity. Just as they were eclectic in their art and their learning, the early Celts perceived themselves to be participants within a total environment in which the cosmic and the human, the natural and the divine, strive towards a visible unity. It is this vision that survives, albeit fitfully, in the Celtic cultures after the decline of the golden age. Of course, not all aspects of Celtic Christianity appeal to us equally today. We have less time for the apocalyptic tradition, which *less appeal* was so strong and in which the Celtic imagination engaged powerfully with Judgement and the end of time. Their severe asceticism can also seem harsh to us. And we are often too optimistic regarding the place of women in Celtic society which, despite the wholesome affirmation of the feminine through powerful female figures such as Brigid, was probably only marginally less patriarchal than other societies of the day. But, finally, we still turn to an earlier age, to the remote margins of north west Europe, and find there precious *possibilities* of Christian consciousness and existence which yet retain their power and which the churches of Christ have neglected for far too long.

A Note on the Selection

The sources for Celtic Christianity are very diverse, and certainly much still remains in manuscript awaiting the attention of editors. The pieces included here represent an attempt to reflect something of that diversity, but the present authors are well aware of the inevitable inadequacy of any such anthology. Much has been left out which others perhaps would have wished to include, but many pieces appear here in new translation, some indeed appearing in English for the first time. In the case of the *Carmina Gadelica*, already well anthologized, Carmichael's own notes have often been included since these cast an important light upon the lived, social context of the pieces. We have also chosen not to emend Carmichael's slightly outdated style in the belief that these self-consciously literary translations have themselves become part of the Celtic inheritance. In the case of the modern poetry, our selection has been pared down due to the substantial costs of reprinting the work of established poets. In making our selection of texts, from all periods, we have chosen the work of authors who either spoke a Celtic language or who can be said to have had a first-hand familiarity with a Celtic-language tradition. Our choice of texts also inevitably reflects our own interests and, unashamedly, the understanding of Celtic Christianity that we have evolved. The fact that an alternative selection of texts could be made which would cast Celtic Christianity in a very different, and probably less positive, light does not undermine the authenticity of our texts but is a reminder that the Celtic tradition we have attempted to identify is more a patterning of spiritual images and ideas than an institutionalized entity with firm boundaries.

Notes

1 This interest is not new. In the late eighteenth century, for instance, the Welsh bard and antiquarian Edward Williams (1747–1826), who is better known by his bardic name, Iolo Morganwg, 'discovered' documents purporting to contain ancient druidic traditions, and on the strength of these writings instituted the 'Gorsedd of the Bards of the Island of Britain'. The *Gorsedd*, consisting of Wales' leading literary figures, still plays a central role in the Welsh National Eisteddfod. In Scotland we have the parallel of James 'Ossian' Macpherson's 'translations' of the Gaelic poetry, published as *Fingal* in 1761, which were also fictitious, owing more to the Romantic Movement than to any extant oral literature. By way of contrast, the serious comparative study of Celtic languages and peoples published by Edward Lhuyd half a century earlier in 1707 (*Archaeologia Britannica*) aroused very little popular interest. It is the *need* to establish links with a Celtic past, real or imagined, which determines the level of public interest and enthusiasm at a particular point in time. (For an account of the search for 'Celticity' in a Scottish context see Malcolm Chapman, *The Gaelic Vision in Scottish Culture*, Croom Helm, London 1978).

2 Colin Renfrew, *Archaeology and Language* (Harmondsworth 1987), pp. 211–249, and Edward Lhuyd (above). The *Grammatica Celtica*, a comparative grammar of the Celtic languages by Johann Kaspar Zeuss, appeared in 1853.

3 See especially Kathleen Hughes, 'The Celtic Church: is this a valid Concept?' in *Cambridge Medieval Celtic Studies* 1 (1981), pp. 1–20 and Wendy Davies, 'The Myth of the Celtic Church' in Nancy Edwards and Alan Lane, eds., *The Early Church in Wales and the West* (Oxbow 1992), pp. 12–21.

4 Matthew Parker, the Archbishop of Canterbury, published his *De Antiquitate Britannicae Ecclesiae* in 1572 in which he argued for a continuity between the British Church in the Celtic period and the Church of the Reformation. This was one of the earliest such works, and many similar volumes were to follow. For an overview of the field, see Glanmor Williams' essay 'Some Protestant Views of Early British Church History' in his *Welsh Reformation Essays* (Cardiff 1967), pp. 207–219.

5 On Celtic society in general, see T. G. E. Powell, *The Celts* (London 1958), Nora Chadwick, *The Celts* (London 1971) and Barry Cunliffe, *The Celtic World* (London 1992).

6 Classical accounts of the Celts are reproduced in J. J. Tierney, *The Celtic Ethnography of Posidonius*, Proceedings of the Royal Irish Academy, Vol. 60, Section C, No. 5 (Dublin 1960), pp.189–275.

7 There are good discussions of Celtic religion in the general studies noted above, to which may be added: Graham Webster, *The British Celts and their Gods under Rome* (London 1986), Jean Louis Brunaux, *The Celtic Gauls: Gods, Rites and Sanctuaries* (English translation London 1988) and Miranda Green, *The Gods of the Celts* (Stroud 1986).

8 Fiona Bowie, 'African Traditional Religions' in *Contemporary Religions: A World Guide*, edited by Ian Harris, Stuart Mews, Paul Morris and John Shepherd (London 1992), pp. 70–72. It is equally possible that the skulls preserved by early Celts were war trophies, kept for their inherent powers (see, for instance, G. W. Trompf, *Melanesian Religion* (Cambridge 1991) pp.45–46).

9 There is more than a hint of the divine possession of bards in the Taliesin tradition, particularly as we find this in the 'druidic' poems from the *Book of Taliesin*. See also Patrick K. Ford's introduction to *Ystoria Taliesin* (Cardiff 1992), and J. E. Caerwyn Williams, *The Irish Literary Tradition* (Cardiff and Belmont, Mass. 1992), pp. 21–49.

10 *Dictionary of the Irish Language*, Royal Irish Academy, s.v. *tuigen*.

11 The Sri Lankan theologian, Aloysius Pieris, has described this process of *inculturation* in which he makes the observation that world (which he calls 'metacosmic') religions spread by fusing with indigenous (or 'cosmic') religions, and are thus to some extent transformed by them.

12 Charles Thomas, *Christianity in Roman Britain to AD 500* (London 1981), pp. 42–50.

13 Ibid., pp. 113–122 and pp. 104–106.

14 M. Forthomme Nicholson seeks to place Pelagius within the Celtic tradition in his article 'Celtic Theology: Pelagius' in James P. Mackey, ed., *An Introduction to Celtic Christianity* (Edinburgh 1989), pp. 386–413.

15 But there is an interesting account in the *Life of Beuno* of how the saint left a disciple *in situ* before fleeing from the advancing Saxons. See also Patrick Sims-Williams, *Religion and Literature in Western England, 600–800* (Cambridge 1990), pp. 79–83 and Charles Thomas, *Christianity in Roman Britain*, pp. 249–294.

16 Kathleen Hughes (ed. D. Dumville), *Celtic Britain in the Early Middle Ages* (Suffolk 1980), pp. 1–21.

17 Dafydd Jenkins, 'Gwalch-Welsh' in *Cambridge Medieval Celtic Studies* 19 (1990), pp. 56–67.

18 Wendy Davies, *Wales in the Early Middle Ages* (Leicester 1982), p. 158.

19 The hermits of the Egyptian desert, Paul of Thebes and Anthony the Great, were popular iconographic figures on High Crosses in Ireland.

20 Nora Chadwick, 'Intellectual Life in West Wales in the Last Days of the Celtic Church' in K. Hughes, C. Brooke, K. Jackson, N. K. Chadwick, eds., *Studies in the Early British Church* (Cambridge 1958), p. 161.

21 A. O. H. Jarman, ed., *Llyfr Du Caerfyrddin* (Cardiff 1982), p. 9.

22 For this and other relevant texts, see Liam de Paor, *St Patrick's World* (Four Courts Press, Co. Dublin 1993), p. 79.

23 Michael Richter, *The Enduring Tradition* (London 1988), p. 95.

24 See Appendix on 'Sources and Acknowledgements', pp. 233–37.

*Medieval Religious
Poetry*

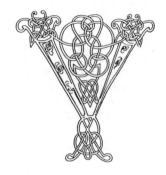

1 *ALMIGHTY CREATOR*

A poem of praise to the Creator in which the poet proclaims his own celebratory gift. It is worth noting the cosmic dimension of the poem and the poet's dismissive attitude to literacy in the third stanza. Circa ninth century. Old Welsh.

Almighty Creator, it is you who have made
the land and the sea . . .

The world cannot comprehend in song bright and melodious,
even though the grass and trees should sing,
all your wonders, O true Lord!

The Father created the world by a miracle;
it is difficult to express its measure.
Letters cannot contain it, letters cannot comprehend it.

Jesus created for the hosts of Christendom,
with miracles when he came,
resurrection through his nature.

He who made the wonder of the world,
will save us, has saved us.
It is not too great a toil to praise the Trinity.

Clear and high in the perfect assembly,
Let us praise above the nine grades of angels
The sublime and blessed Trinity.

Purely, humbly, in skilful verse,
I should love to give praise to the Trinity,
according to the greatness of his power.

God has required of the host in this world
who are his, that they should at all times,
all together, fear the Trinity.

The one who has power, wisdom and dominion
above heaven, below heaven, completely;
it is not too great toil to praise the Son of Mary.

2 GLORIOUS LORD

Another cosmic poem of praise in which the author shows an awareness of his own role as praise-poet. This poem is evidently dependent upon Psalm 148 or the Benedicite of Daniel 3.23ff, or both. The 'three springs'—sun, moon and sea—of line 5 belong to native Celtic cosmology. We should note also the combination of motifs from the world of nature, human society and the Church. Tenth to eleventh century. Early Middle Welsh.

Hail to you, glorious Lord!
May church and chancel praise you,
May chancel and church praise you,
May plain and hillside praise you,
May the three springs praise you,
Two higher than the wind and one above the earth,
May darkness and light praise you,
May the cedar and sweet fruit-tree praise you.
Abraham praised you, the founder of faith,
May life everlasting praise you,
May the birds and the bees praise you,
May the stubble and the grass praise you.
Aaron and Moses praised you,
May male and female praise you,
May the seven days and the stars praise you,
May the lower and upper air praise you,
May books and letters praise you,
May the fish in the river praise you,
May thought and action praise you,
May the sand and the earth praise you,
May all the good things created praise you,
And I too shall praise you, Lord of glory,
Hail to you, glorious Lord!

3 *THE SCRIBE IN THE WOODS*

The following was written in the margin of a manuscript of the Latin grammarian Priscian, which was copied by Irish monks at St Gall in the first half of the ninth century. Old Irish.

A hedge of trees surrounds me, a blackbird's lay sings to me, praise I
    shall not conceal,
Above my lined book the trilling of the birds sings to me.
A clear-voiced cuckoo sings to me in a grey cloak from the tops of
    bushes,
May the Lord save me from Judgement; well do I write under the
    greenwood.

4 *A HYMN OF PRAISE*

The ultimate origin of these stanzas is the doxology found in Revelation 7.12, where we are told that the angels who surround the throne of God worship him and sing: 'Praise and glory and wisdom, thanksgiving and honour, power and might, be to our God for ever and ever.' Circa ninth century. Old Irish.

Blessing and brightness,
Wisdom, thanksgiving,
Great power and might
To the King who rules over all.

Glory and honour and goodwill,
Praise and the sublime song of minstrels,
Overflowing love from every heart
To the King of Heaven and Earth.

To the chosen Trinity has been joined
Before all, after all, universal
Blessing and everlasting blessing,
Blessing everlasting and blessing.

5 *THE LORD OF CREATION*

This beautifully crafted poem dates from the ninth century. Old Irish.

Let us adore the Lord,
Maker of marvellous works,
Bright heaven with its angels,
And on earth the white-waved sea.

6 *PRAISE TO THE TRINITY*

This is a hymn which may possibly have had some kind of para-liturgical usage. Again the cosmic dimension of praise is stressed, as is God the Creator. The reference at the end of the second stanza is to Paul of Thebes and Anthony the Great, two early Fathers of the Egyptian desert. In this poem we again see the interweaving of the social, natural and Christian world. The 'five cities' are the 'cities of the plain', which include Sodom and Gomorrah from Genesis 9.29. Tenth to eleventh century. Early Middle Welsh.

I praise the threefold
Trinity as God,
Who is one and three,
A single power in unity,
His attributes a single mystery,
One God to praise.
Great King, I praise you,
Great your glory.
Your praise is true;
I am the one who praises you.
Poetry's welfare
Is in Elohim's care.
Hail to you, O Christ,
Father, Son
And Holy Ghost,
Our Adonai.

I praise two,
Who is one and two,

Who is truly three,
To doubt him is not easy,
Who made fruit and flowing water
And all variety,
God is his name as two,
Godly his words,
God is his name as three,
Godly his power,
God is his name as one,
The God of Paul and Anthony.

I praise the one,
Who is two and one,
Who is three together,
Who is God himself,
He made Mars and Luna.
Man and woman,
The difference in sound between
Shallow water and the deep.
He made the hot and the cold,
The sun and the moon,
The word in the tablet,
And the flame in the taper,
Love in our senses,
A girl, dear and tender,
And burned five cities
Because of false union.

7 PRAISE TO GOD

In the following poem Christ is depicted as a conquering hero, and the text consciously imitates the language of the secular heroic tradition. Words denoting action and achievement are repeatedly used. In the 'perfect rite' and the anticipation of the 'feast . . . in Paradise' there also seem to be echoes of the Eucharistic sacrifice. The opening phrase of the poem, with its mix of Welsh and Latin, also has specifically liturgical associations. The theological erudition of the poem suggests that its author may well have been a priest. Tenth to eleventh century. Early Middle Welsh.

In the name of the Lord, mine to praise, of great praise,
I shall praise God, great the triumph of his love,
God who defended us, God who made us, God who saved us,
God our hope, perfect and honourable, beautiful his blessing.
We are in God's power, God above, Trinity's king.
God proved himself our liberation by his suffering,
God came to be imprisoned in humility.
Wise Lord, who will free us by Judgement Day,
Who will lead us to the feast through his mercy and sanctity
In Paradise, in pure release from the burden of sin,
Who will bring us salvation through penance and the five wounds.
Terrible grief, God defended us when he took on flesh.
Man would be lost if the perfect rite had not redeemed him.
Through the cross, blood-stained, came salvation to the world.
Christ, strong shepherd, his honour shall not fail.

8 PRAISING GOD AT THE BEGINNING AND END

This poem shows a typical concern with the inevitability of death, and is an appeal to God for mercy. The poet urges his monastic audience to follow their ascetical lifestyle more vigorously. Tenth to eleventh century. Early Middle Welsh.

He shall not refuse or reject whoever strives
To praise God at the beginning and end of the day,
Mary's only son, the Lord of kings.
Like the sun he shall come, from east to north.
Mary, Christ's mother, chief of maidens,
Call for the sake of your great mercy
Upon your son to chase away our sin.
God above us, God before us, may the God who rules,
Heaven's king, grant us a share of his mercy.
Royal-hearted one, peace between us
Without rejection, may I make amends
For the wrong I have done before going
To my tomb, my green grave,
My place of rest, in the dark without candle,
My burial place, my recess, my repose,

After enjoying the horses and new mead,
Feasting and women's company.
I shall not sleep; I shall consider my end.
We live in a world of wretched vanity,
Which shall pass away like leaves from a tree.
Woe to the miser who gathers great wealth.
Though the world's course lets him be,
He shall, unless he gives all to God,
Face peril at his end.
The fool does not know how to tremble in his heart,
Nor to rise early in the morning, pray and prostrate,
Nor to chant prayers or petition mercy.
He will pay in the end bitterly
For his pomp, his pride and arrogance.
For the toads and snakes he feeds his body,
And for lions, and he performs iniquity,
But death shall enter in and greedily
Devour him, bearing him away.
Old age draws near and senility;
Your hearing, your sight, your teeth grow weak,
And the skin of your fingers is wrinkly,
It is old age and grey hairs that cause this.
May Michael intercede for us with the Lord of Heaven
For a share of his mercy.

9 GRANT ME TEARS, O LORD

The tears of compunction are the theme of this poem, which underlines the extent to which the true monastic vocation is based on personal conversion and repentance. Circa tenth century, or later. Old Irish, with later features.

Grant me tears, O Lord, to blot out my sins; may I not cease from them, O God, until I have been purified.

May my heart be burned by the fire of redemption; grant me tears with purity for Mary and Íte.

When I contemplate my sins, grant me tears always, for great are the claims of tears on cheeks.

Grant me tears when rising, grant me tears when resting, beyond your every gift altogether for love of you, Mary's Son.

Grant me tears in bed to moisten my pillow, so that his dear ones may help to cure the soul.

Grant me contrition of heart so that I may not be in disgrace; O Lord, protect me and grant me tears.

For the dalliance I had with women, who did not reject me, grant me tears, O Creator, flowing in streams from my eyes.

For my anger and my jealousy and my pride, a foolish deed, in pools from my inmost parts bring forth tears.

My falsehoods and my lying and my greed, grievous the three, to banish them all from me, O Mary, grant me tears.

10 *ALL ALONE IN MY LITTLE CELL*

This poem conveys the spirit of asceticism that motivated many of the early monks. Death is here pictured both as the inevitable end of life, and as a release from sin and penance. Eighth or ninth century. Old Irish.

All alone in my little cell, without the company of a single person; precious has been the pilgrimage before going to meet death.

A hidden secluded little hut, for the forgiveness of my sins: an upright, untroubled conscience towards holy heaven.

Sanctifying the body by good habits, trampling like a man upon it: with weak and tearful eyes for the forgiveness of my passions.

Passions weak and withered, renouncing this wretched world; pure and eager thoughts; let this be a prayer to God.

Heartfelt lament towards cloudy heaven, sincere and truly devout confessions, swift showers of tears.

A cold and anxious bed, like the lying down of a doomed man: a brief, apprehensive sleep; invocations frequent and early.

My food as befits my station, precious has been the captivity: my dinner, without doubt, would not make me full-blooded.

Dry bread weighed out, well we bow the head; water of the many-coloured hillside, that is the drink I would take.

A bitter meagre dinner; diligently feeding the sick; keeping off strife and visits; a calm, serene conscience.

It would be desirable, a pure and holy blemish: cheeks withered and sunken, a shrivelled leathery skin.

Treading the paths of the gospel; singing psalms at every Hour; an end of talking and long stories; constant bending of knees.

May my Creator visit me, my Lord, my King; may my spirit seek him in the everlasting kingdom in which he is.

Let this be the end of vice in the enclosures of churches; a lovely little cell among the graves, and I alone therein.

All alone in my little cell, all alone thus; alone I came into the world, alone I shall go from it.

If on my own I have sinned through pride of this world, hear me wail for it all alone, O God!

11 *ON THE FLIGHTINESS OF THOUGHT*

This poem is taken from the manuscript known as the Leabhar Breac, *or 'Speckled Book' of the early fifteenth century. The poem again conveys the theme of monastic repentance as the monk regrets the inconstancy of his thought and entreats God to save him. The sevenfold Spirit is a reference to the gifts of the Holy Spirit, which are the virtues. Circa tenth century. Middle Irish.*

Shame on my thoughts, how they stray from me! I fear great danger
from this on the Day of Eternal Judgement.

During the psalms they wander on a path that is not right: they run,
they distract, they misbehave before the eyes of the great God.

Through eager gatherings, through companies of lewd wowen,
through woods, through cities — swifter they are than the wind.

One moment they follow ways of loveliness, and the next ways of
riotous shame — no lie!

Without a ferry or a false step they cross every sea: swiftly they leap
in one bound from earth to heaven.

They run — not a course of great wisdom — near, far: following paths
along paths of great foolishness they reach their home.

Though one should try to bind them or put shackles on their feet,
they are neither constant nor inclined to rest a while.

Neither the edge of a sword nor the stripe of lash will subdue them;
as slippery as an eel's tale they elude my grasp.

Neither lock nor well-constructed dungeon, nor any fetter on earth,
neither stronghold nor sea nor bleak fastness restrains them from
their course.

O beloved truly chaste Christ, to whom every eye is clear, may the
grace of the sevenfold Spirit come to keep them, to hold them in
check!

Rule this heart of mind, O swift God of the elements, that you may
be my love, and that I may do your will!

That I may reach Christ with his chosen companions, that we may
be together: they are neither fickle nor inconstant — they are not
as I am.

12 *MAYTIME IS THE FAIREST SEASON*

The author of this poem again contemplates death and the fragility of life. His 'brothers' are probably his fellow-monks who may also be members of his own family. Tenth to eleventh century. Early Middle Welsh.

Maytime is the fairest season,
With its loud bird-song and green trees,
When the plough is in the furrow
And the oxen under the yoke,
When the sea is green,
And the land many colours.

But when cuckoos sing on the tops
Of the lovely trees, my sadness deepens,
The smoke stings and my grief is clear
Since my brothers have passed away.

On the hill and in the valley,
On the islands of the sea,
Whichever path you take,
You shall not hide from blessed Christ.

It was our wish, our Brother, our way,
To go to the land of your exile.
Seven saints and seven score and seven hundred
Went to the one court with blessed Christ,
And were without fear.

The gift I ask, may it not be denied me,
Is peace between myself and God.
May I find the way to the gate of glory,
May I not be sad, O Christ, in your court.

13 *THE PATH I WALK*

This very early accentual poem survives in a fifteenth century manuscript where it is attributed to Colum Cille: 'This is the protection of Colum Cille. And it is to be said at bed-time and on rising, and when going on a journey, and is of marvellous avail.' It is full of the language of trade and, whether by Colum Cille or not, may reflect the experience of a pilgrim priest, seeking souls for God. Sixth to eighth century. Old Irish.

The path I walk, Christ walks it. May the land in which I am be without
    sorrow.
May the Trinity protect me wherever I stay, Father, Son and Holy
    Spirit.
Bright angels walk with me — dear presence — in every dealing.
In every dealing I pray them that no one's poison may reach me.
The ninefold people of heaven of holy cloud, the tenth force of the stout
    earth.
Favourable company, they come with me, so that the Lord may not be
    angry with me.
May I arrive at every place, may I return home; may the way in which I
    spend be a way without loss.
May every path before me be smooth, man, woman and child welcome
    me.
A truly good journey! Well does the fair Lord show us a course, a path.

14 *MAY THIS JOURNEY BE EASY*

The following is a blessing for a journey. Tenth century or later. Middle Irish.

May this journey be easy, may it be a journey of profit in my hands!
    Holy Christ against demons, against weapons, against killings!

May Jesus and the Father, may the Holy Spirit sanctify us!
May the mysterious God be not hidden in darkness, may the bright
    King save us!

May the cross of Christ's body and Mary guard us on the road!
May it not be unlucky for us, may it be successful and easy!

15 *THE SAINTS' CALENDAR OF ADOMNÁN*

The following is a prayer to the saints who preside over the different seasons. Adomnán, to whom the work is attributed in one manuscript tradition, was the

ninth abbot of Iona and the author of the Life of Columba. *'God's fosterling'
is a reference to Christ, and the 'other calendar' is that of Oengus, with which
the poet favourably compares his own. The final stanza may be a later addition.
Old Irish, with some Middle Irish forms.*

The saints of the four seasons,
I long to pray to them,
May they save me from torments,
The saints of the whole year!

The saints of the glorious springtime,
May they be with me
By the will
Of God's fosterling.

The saints of the dry summer,
About them is my poetic frenzy,
That I may come from this land
To Jesus, son of Mary.

The saints of the beautiful autumn,
I call upon a company not unharmonious,
That they may draw near to me,
With Mary and Michael.

The saints of the winter I pray to,
May they be with me against the throng of demons,
Around Jesus of the mansions,
The Sprit holy, heavenly.

The other calendar,
Which noble saints will have,
Though it has more verses,
It does not have more saints.

I beseech the saints of the earth,
I beseech all the angels,
I beseech God himself, both when rising and lying down,
Whatever I do or say, that I may dwell in the heavenly land.

16 *A PRAYER TO THE ARCHANGELS FOR EVERY DAY OF THE WEEK*

This early poem again invokes supernatural protection and well shows the importance of the Archangels to the early medieval Irish mind, as beings who exercised benign influence upon human life. Circa ninth century. Old Irish.

May Gabriel be with me on Sundays, and the power of the King of
    Heaven.
May Gabriel be with me always that evil may not come to me nor injury.

Michael on Monday I speak of, my mind is set on him,
Not with anyone do I compare him but with Jesus, Mary's son.

If it be Tuesday, Raphael I mention, until the end comes, for my help.
One of the seven whom I beseech, as long as I am on the field of the
    world.

May Uriel be with me on Wednesdays, the abbot with high nobility,
Against wound and against danger, against the sea of rough wind.

Sariel on Thursday I speak of, against the swift waves of the sea,
Against every evil that comes to a man, against every disease that seizes
    him.

On the day of the second fast, Rumiel — a clear blessing — I have loved,
I say only the truth, good the friend I have taken.

May Panchel be with me on Saturdays, as long as I am in the yellow-
    coloured world,
May sweet Mary, together with her friend, deliver me from strangers.

May the Trinity protect me! May the Trinity defend me!
May the Trinity save me from every hurt, from every danger.

17 *THREE WISHES I ASK*

This short poem is beautifully expressive of the spirit of renunciation which characterized early Irish monasticism. Circa ninth century. Old Irish.

Three wishes I ask of the King when I part from my body: may I have nothing to confess, may I have no enemy, may I own nothing!

Three wishes I ask this day of the King, ruler of suns: may I have no dignity or honours that may lead me into torment!

May I do no work without reward before the Christ of this world! May God take my soul when it is most pure! Finally, may I not be guilty when my three wishes have been spoken!

18 ST PATRICK'S BREASTPLATE

The following stanzas are from a text which has long been attributed to St Patrick and is sometimes known as The Deer's Cry. *It actually dates in its present form from a period several centuries after the death of the saint and it is the classic example of a* Lorica *or 'breastplate' prayer which invokes divine protection for the speaker's life and body. This is an ancient monastic practice which reflects the words of St Paul in Ephesians 6.11–18. Eighth century. Old Irish.*

> I rise today
>> in power's strength, invoking the Trinity,
>> believing in threeness,
>> confessing the oneness,
>> of creation's Creator.

> I rise today
>> in the power of Christ's birth and baptism,
>> in the power of his crucifixion and burial,
>> in the power of his rising and ascending,
>> in the power of his descending and judging.

> I rise today
>> in the power of the love of cherubim,
>> in the obedience of angels
>> and service of archangels,
>> in hope of rising to receive the reward,
>> in the prayers of patriarchs,
>> in the predictions of prophets,

in the preaching of apostles,
in the faith of confessors,
in the innocence of holy virgins,
in the deeds of the righteous.

I rise today
    in heaven's might,
    in sun's brightness,
    in moon's radiance,
    in fire's glory,
    in lightning's quickness,
    in wind's swiftness,
    in sea's depth,
    in earth's stability,
    in rock's fixity.

I rise today
    with the power of God to pilot me,
    God's strength to sustain me,
    God's wisdom to guide me,
    God's eye to look ahead for me,
    God's ear to hear me,
    God's word to speak for me,
    God's hand to protect me,
    God's way before me,
    God's shield to defend me,
    God's host to deliver me:
        from snares of devils,
        from evil temptations,
        from nature's failings,
        from all who wish to harm me,
        far or near,
        alone and in a crowd.

Around me I gather today all these powers
    against every cruel and merciless force
    to attack my body and soul,
    against the charms of false prophets,
    the black laws of paganism,
    the false laws of heretics,

the deceptions of idolatry,
against spells cast by women, smiths and druids,
and all unlawful knowledge
that harms the body and soul.

May Christ protect me today
against poison and burning,
against drowning and wounding,
so that I may have abundant reward;
Christ with me, Christ before me, Christ behind me;
Christ within me, Christ beneath me, Christ above me;
Christ to right of me, Christ to left of me;
Christ in my lying, Christ in my sitting, Christ in my rising;
Christ in the heart of all who think of me,
Christ on the tongue of all who speak to me,
Christ in the eye of all who see me,
Christ in the ear of all who hear me.

I rise today
in power's strength, invoking the Trinity,
believing in threeness,
confessing the oneness,
of creation's Creator.

For to the Lord belongs salvation,
and to the Lord belongs salvation
and to Christ belongs salvation.

May your salvation, Lord, be with us always.

19 *ALEXANDER'S BREASTPLATE*

The following poem is described as a Lorica, *or 'breastplate', and is —
wrongly — attributed to Alexander the Great, whose exploits were made
known in the medieval world through the writings of the historian Orosius.
The poem is typical in its evocation of the power of Christ as a defence against all
ills. Twelfth or thirteenth century. Middle Welsh.*

On the face of the world
There was not born
His equal.
Three-person God,
Trinity's only Son,
Gentle and strong.
Son of the Godhead,
Son of humanity,
Only Son of wonder.
The Son of God is a refuge,
Mary's Son a blessed sanctuary,
A noble child was seen.
Great his splendour,
Great Lord and God,
In the place of glory.
From the line of Adam
And Abraham
We were born.
From David's line,
The fulfilment of prophecy,
The host was born again.
By his word he saved the blind and the deaf,
From all suffering,
The ragged,
Foolish sinners,
And those of impure mind.
Let us rise up
To meet the Trinity,
Following our salvation.
Christ's cross is bright,
A shining breastplate
Against all harm,
Against all our enemies may it be strong:
The place of our protection.

20 THE HOLY MAN

These words occur on the margin of Codex S. Pauli *and are spoken by the Devil to St Moling. Eighth century. Old Irish.*

He is a bird round which a trap closes,
He is a leaky ship to which peril is dangerous,
He is an empty vessel, he is a withered tree,
Whoever does not do the will of the King above.
He is pure gold, he is the radiance round the sun,
He is a vessel of silver with wine,
He is happy, beautiful and holy,
Whoever does the will of the King.

21 PRAYER

From the Litany of Confession. The place of litanies in early Irish devotional and liturgical life is unclear, but there are a significant number of such texts written in both Latin and Irish. The following has been attributed to the sixth century saint, Ciaran of Clonmacnois, but must date from a later period. The first line is Latin, otherwise Irish.

'According to the multitude of your mercies, cleanse my iniquity.'

O star-like sun,
O guiding light,
O home of the planets,
O fiery-maned and marvellous one,
O fertile, undulating, fiery sea,
            Forgive.

O fiery glow,
O fiery flame of Judgement,
            Forgive.

O holy story-teller, holy scholar,
O full of holy grace, of holy strength,
O overflowing, loving, silent one,
O generous and thunderous giver of gifts,
            Forgive.

O rock-like warrior of a hundred hosts,
O fair crowned one, victorious, skilled in battle,
            Forgive.

45

22 NININE'S PRAYER

This prayer is traditionally attributed to the poet Ninine or to Fiacc, Bishop of Sletty. It occurs in the eleventh century Irish Book of Hymns, but is of earlier date. It is a fine example of the place of the saints in the devotional life of the early Celts. Old Irish.

We invoke holy Patrick, Ireland's chief apostle.
Glorious is his marvellous name, a flame that baptized heathen.
He warred against hard-hearted druids.
He thrust down the proud with the help of our Lord of fair heaven.
He cleansed Ireland's meadowlands, a great birth.
We pray to Patrick, chief apostle; his judgement shall save us on
    Doomsday from the evil of dark devils.
God be with us, and the prayer of Patrick, chief apostle.

23 PRAYER

This prayer is traditionally attributed to the Columbanus (c.543–615), although the attribution is doubted. Latin.

O Lord God, destroy and root out whatever the Adversary plants in me, that with my sins destroyed you may sow understanding and good work in my mouth and heart; so that in act and in truth I may serve only you and know how to fulfil the commandments of Christ and to seek yourself. Give me memory, give me love, give me chastity, give me faith, give me all things which you know belong to the profit of my soul. O Lord, work good in me, and provide me with what you know that I need. Amen.

24 LITANY OF THE VIRGIN AND ALL SAINTS

The following litany includes references to the organs of sense, as the places where sin occurs, and is thus reminiscent of the tradition of the 'breastplate'. It reflects a monastic and celibate milieu and occurs in manuscripts of the fifteenth century, though it may be earlier.

May Mary and John the youth and John the Baptist and all the saints of the world intercede with the fount of true purity and true innocence, Jesus Christ, Son of the Virgin, that the grace and compassion of the Holy Spirit may come to forgive us all our past sins, and protect us from future sins, to subdue our fleshly desires, and to control our unseemly thoughts;

> To kindle the love and affection of the Creator in our hearts, that it may be he that our mind searches for, desires and meditates upon for ever;
>
> That our eyes may not be deceived by idle glances, and by the profitless beauty of perishable things;
>
> That our hearing may not be perverted by idle songs, nor by the harmful persuasion of devils and evil men.
>
> That our senses of taste may not be beguiled by dainties and many savours.
>
> That he may free our tongues from denigration and insult and unkind chatter.
>
> That we may not barter the true light and true beauty of the life eternal for the deceitful fantasy of the present life.
>
> That we may not forsake the pure wedlock and marriage of our husband and noble bridegroom, Jesus Christ, Son of the King of Heaven and Earth, for the impure wedlock of a servant of his, so that our soul and body may be a consecrated temple to the Holy Spirit,
>
> That we may accompany the blameless lamb,
>
> That we may sing the song that only the virgins sing,
>
> That we may merit the crown of eternal glory in the unity of the company of heaven, in the presence of the Trinity, for ever and ever. Amen.

25 MY SPEECH — MAY IT PRAISE YOU

This poem expresses the author's desire to praise God in perfect form. Note the triadic structure. Twelfth century or later. Middle Irish.

My speech — may it praise you without flaw: may my heart love you, King of Heaven and of earth.

My speech — may it praise you without flaw: make it easy for me, pure Lord, to do you all service and to adore you.

My speech — may it praise you without flaw: Father of all affection,
   hear my poems and my speech.

26 *TO THE TRINITY*

*The theme of death again dominates this poem, and the poet speculates whether
he will be found worthy on the Day of Judgement. His religious task in this life
is to sing the praises of God and to entreat his mercy, and it is this that will
finally give him a place in 'the land of Heaven'. Twelfth or thirteenth century.
Middle Welsh.*

To the Trinity I make my prayer,
O Lord, grant me the skill to sing your praise,
For the way of this world is perilous,
Our deeds and decisions a wild tumult.
Among the family of the saints, in their society,
King of Heaven, may I be ready to praise you.
Before my soul parts from my body,
Grant me, for my sins, the means to worship you,
To sing entreaty before your glory.
May I be part of the merciful Trinity,
My plea to you is like a battle cry,
Nine orders of heaven, he made the hosts,
The tenth is the blessed company of the saints,
Wonderful glory of the peoples,
A great host, their noble victory is clear,
A company who see God . . .
In heaven, on earth, at my end,
In times of joy and sorrow, in tribulation,
In my body, in my soul, in austerity,
Long preparation before the approach of glory,
I shall beseech you, Lord of the land of peace,
That my soul may dwell
For all eternity, in the highest place,
In the land of heaven, I shall not be refused.

27 THE DEATHBED SONG OF MEILYR BRYDYDD

Meilyr Brydydd was the first of the 'Poets of the Princes'. He was court poet to Gruffudd ap Cynan, the prince most closely associated with the rise of the province of Gwynedd in North Wales. In this poem he reflects upon the inevitability of his own death, and entreats God for his mercy. Enlli, or Bardsey Island, was a major centre of pilgrimage, where 20,000 saints were reputed to be buried. Early twelfth century. Middle Welsh.

King of kings, leader easy to praise,
I ask this favour of my highest Lord:
Realm-mastering ruler of the sublime and blessed land,
Noble chief, make peace between you and me.
Feeble and empty is my mind, since
I have provoked you, and full of regret.
I have sinned before the Lord my God,
Failing to attend to my due devotion;
But I shall serve my Lord King
Before I am laid in the earth, stripped of life.
A true foretelling (to Adam and his offspring
The prophets had declared
That Jesus would be in the womb of martyrs),
Mary gladly received her burden.
But a burden I have amassed of unclean sin
And have been shaken by its clamour.
Lord of all places, how good you are to praise,
May I praise you and be purified before punishment.
King of all kings, who know me, do not refuse me,
On account of wickedness, for the sake of your mercy.
Many a time I had gold and brocade
From fickle kings for praising them,
And after the gift of song of a superior power,
Poverty-stricken is my tongue on the prospect of its silence.
I am Meilyr the Poet, pilgrim to Peter,
Gate-keeper who measures right virtue.
When the time of our resurrection comes,
All who are in the grave, make me ready.
As I await the call, may my home be
The monastery where the tide rises,

49

A wilderness of enduring glory,
Around its cemetery the breast of the sea,
Island of fair Mary, sacred isle of the saints,
Awaiting resurrection there is lovely.
Christ of the prophesied cross, who knows me, shall guide me
Past hell, the isolated abode of agony.
The Creator who made me shall receive me
Among the pure parish, the people of Enlli.

28 MEILYR AP GWALCHMAI'S ODE TO GOD

The following stanzas are taken from a poem by Meilyr ap Gwalchmai, who came from Anglesey and was the grandson of Meilyr Brydydd. We again see the poet's sense that his own salvation depends upon the proper use of his art: 'May being righteous on account of my gift cleanse me.' In fact, by his use of imagery, the poet deftly succeeds in identifying faith as right or 'skilled' belief, with the 'skills' of his poetic art, and the divine 'gift' of grace with the 'gift' of his inspiration and art. Late twelfth century. Middle Welsh.

May God grant me, may I be granted mercy,
May no evil lack defeat me,
May being righteous on account of my gift cleanse me
And the world, which I know well, be shaken.
May I deserve God's favour, the Lord glorify me,
And give me entrance to the home of heaven.

Heaven shall be sure for those who seek freely
The royal growth of the religion of the Creed.
May the king of seas and stars hear me,
Privileged is the cause of one who petitions.
May the honour of the land of Paradise admit me;
That is the genuine kingdom and true.

With fullness of wisdom may my spirit reflect
On the wise fusion of skills that shall make me skilful.
A skilled man does not approach him who speaks
The glib and lying word, for all he may preach it.
I believe in Christ, blessed teacher,
No skilled believer it is who does not believe in him.

May I believe and reflect, and may the wise one see that
I believe in God and the saints and their land's honour,
A Christian am I with unshakeable right to a gift;
Christ, may I be granted gifts when he gives.
May Christianity's nurture release me,
The Lord Christ my King bring me freedom.

And may heaven's king protect me from error;
May his gift and his understanding cure my faults.
May God, who is flawless, not destroy me;
Undarkened is the mind that praises him,
Undeceived is the love that loves him,
Unblemished glory for all who believe in him.

May God, creator and ruler, guide me till judgement,
May he desire the ways of sinlessness for me,
And may it be his majestic desire to give me
Bright gifts that can purify me:
May rites of remission accompany my end,
And gifts of counsel guide me.

The counsellor of man, gentle to all who desire him,
Bears no ill-will to those who love him.
Love for me it is that can clear my blame;
May love and his concern for me not fail.
May the friend of our true cause elect me,
May I have the friendship of the Lord for ever.

29 THE DEATHBED SONG OF CYNDDELW
THE GREAT POET

Cynddelw, from Powys in mid-Wales, is generally regarded as the greatest of the 'Poets of the Princes'. In these stanzas from the Black Book *Cynddelw shows again that the poet wins salvation through the quality of his praise and the skill of his verse, both of which have their source in God. Late twelfth century. Middle Welsh.*

Greatest Lord, take to yourself
This tribute of praise and well-formed poetry.

Perfect is the speech-skill and shape
Of my extolling song, candle of a hundred lands;
For you are master and great monarch,
You are counsellor and light's lord,
You are the heart of the prophet, and judge,
You are my generous ruler, the giver,
You are teacher to me; drive me not from your heights,
In your wrath, or from your lovely land,
Nor deny me your favour, my Lord Creator,
Nor refuse my submission and lowly plea.
Nor deliver me by your hand to a wretched home,
Nor let me run with the black host of the rejected.

Greatest Lord, when I sang of you,
Not without worth were my words,
Nor bereft of fair features,
Not wanting the grace wherever I received it.
Unshakeable God did not make me
To pursue folly, deceit or violence.
Such a one, I considered, shall not be woken,
Nor be given heaven, who seeks it not.
I did not serve too keenly,
Nor profit too greatly,
Nor let arrogance grow in my breast,
Nor did I pursue too much penance,
But to be in my Lord's dwelling was my desire,
And freedom for the soul, the need for which I prayed.

30 FRAGMENT OF THE DISPUTE BETWEEN BODY AND SOUL

These stanzas are part of a lost dialogue poem of a type found in many different cultures in medieval Europe. Normally, the soul castigates the body as the seat of sin. In this case however the body takes its rightful place beside the soul as its 'companion in glory'—since physical penance is the path to Heaven. Tenth to eleventh century. Early Middle Welsh.

While we walk together, companion in glory,
Be perfect in what you do.

Let us seek salvation
Through faith, religion and creed.

Companions in faith, by the friendship of faith
Comes great and long penance daily;
Soul, when you ask me what my end shall be:
The grave or eternity.

31 THE MASS OF THE GROVE

This poem was written in the fourteenth century by Dafydd ap Gwilym, who is widely regarded as the greatest Welsh poet. It presents a delicate fusion of natural imagery and Christian liturgy, as well as touches of courtly love. Morfudd here is the name of the poet's beloved. The 'englyn' referred to in the fifth line is a type of short Welsh poem in strict metre. It is the lyrical cock thrush who is the central figure; and he will return in a much later poem entitled 'The Mistle Thrush' given below. Middle Welsh.

I was in a pleasant place today
Beneath mantles of fine, green hazel,
Listening at break of day
To the skilful cock thrush
Singing a splendid englyn
Of fluent signs and lessons.
He is a stranger here, of wise nature,
Love's brown go-between from afar,
From fair Carmarthenshire he came
At my golden girl's command.
Full of words, without password,
He makes his way to Nentyrch valley;
It was Morfudd who sent him,
Foster son of May, skilled in the arts of song,
Swathed in the vestments
Of flowers of the sweet boughs of May,
His chasuble was of the wings,
Green mantles of the wind.
By the great God, there was here
Only gold for the altar's canopy.
In bright language I heard

A long and faultless chanting,
An unfaltering reading to the people
Of the gospel without haste,
And on the hill for us there
Was raised a well-formed leaf as wafer,
And the slender, eloquent nightingale
From the corner of a nearby grove,
Poetess of the valley, rings out to the many
The Sanctus bell in her clear whistle,
Raising the sacrifice on high
To the sky above the bush,
With adoration to God the Father,
And with a chalice of ecstasy and love.
This psalmody pleases me:
Bred it was by a gentle grove of birch trees.

32 *THE LOVES OF TALIESIN*

This is one of the greatest works of medieval Welsh religious literature. It conveys a comprehensive view of human life by interweaving the social, natural and religious worlds. Penance, and the desire for penance, which is the thematic heart of the poem, seems remarkably free of the negative connotations it generally bears in the modern world. Penance, rather, is the possibility of glory. Circa thirteenth century. Middle Welsh.

The beauty of the virtue in doing penance for excess,
Beautiful too that God shall save me.
The beauty of a companion who does not deny me his company,
Beautiful too the drinking horn's society.
The beauty of a master like Nudd, the wolf of God,
Beautiful too a man who is noble, kind and generous.
The beauty of berries at harvest time,
Beautiful too the grain on the stalk.
The beauty of the sun, clear in the sky,
Beautiful too they who pay Adam's debt.
The beauty of a herd's thick-maned stallion,
Beautiful too the pattern of his plaits.
The beauty of desire and a silver ring,
Beautiful too a ring for a virgin.

The beauty of an eagle on the shore when tide is full,
Beautiful too the seagulls playing.
The beauty of a horse and gold-trimmed shield,
Beautiful too a bold man in the breach.
The beauty of Einion, healer of many,
Beautiful too a generous and obliging minstrel.
The beauty of May with its cuckoo and nightingale,
Beautiful too when good weather comes.
The beauty of a proper and perfect wedding feast,
Beautiful too a gift which is loved.
The beauty of desire for penance from a priest,
Beautiful too bearing the elements to the altar.
The beauty for a minstrel of mead at the head of the hall,
Beautiful too a lively crowd surrounding a hero.
The beauty of a faithful priest in his church,
Beautiful too a chieftain in his hall.
The beauty of a strong parish led by God,
Beautiful too being in the season of Paradise.
The beauty of the moon shining on the earth,
Beautiful too when your luck is good.
The beauty of summer, its days long and slow,
Beautiful too visiting the ones we love.
The beauty of flowers on the tops of fruit trees,
Beautiful too covenant with the Creator.
The beauty in the wilderness of doe and fawn,
Beautiful too the foam-mouthed and slender steed.
The beauty of the garden when the leeks grow well,
Beautiful too the charlock in bloom.
The beauty of the horse in its leather halter,
Beautiful too keeping company with a king.
The beauty of a hero who does not shun injury,
Beautiful too is elegant Welsh.
The beauty of the heather when it turns purple,
Beautiful too moorland for cattle.
The beauty of the season when calves suckle,
Beautiful too riding a foam-mouthed horse.
And for me there is no less beauty
In the father of the horn in a feast of mead.
The beauty of the fish in his bright lake,
Beautiful too its surface shimmering.

The beauty of the word which the Trinity speaks,
Beautiful too doing penance for sin.
But the loveliest of all is covenant
With God on the Day of Judgement.

33 *from* 'THE MIRROR OF DEATH'

The following is from a sixteenth century Breton poem by Mestre Jehan an Archer Coz entitled 'The Mirror of Death'. It well shows the fascination with the brevity of life and certainty of divine judgement which is so characteristic of Celtic writings. Middle Breton.

Birds are caught in snares during the time of ice, when they are in search of food, and fish are caught in nets, and, though they had never thought of dying, are now being cooked for supper over the charcoal fire. Such is your life too, from beginning to end, which you spend in this world in the midst of many sins, and if you do not put them right before your time comes after all your pleasures, then you will remain caught in the snares . . .

34 *from* 'THE MISTLE THRUSH'

Thomas Jones (1756–1820) was an early Methodist minister. A close friend of Thomas Charles, he was a leading author and figure in eighteenth century Wales. Although written by a convinced Calvinist, the interpenetration of the themes of nature and grace that we find in the following poem seems to owe as much to the spirit of medieval poets such as Dafydd ap Gwilym and Rhys Goch ap Rhiccert as it does to the theology of Geneva.

Lowly bird, beautifully taught,
You enrich and astound us,
We wonder long at your song,
Your artistry and your voice.
In you I see, I believe,
The clear and excellent work of God.
Blessed and glorious is he,
Who shows his virtue in the lowest kind.
How many bright wonders (clear note of loveliness)

Does this world contain?
How many parts, how many mirrors of his finest work
Offer themselves a hundred times to our gaze?
For the book of his art is a speaking light
Of lines abundantly full,
And every day one chapter after another
Comes among us to teach us of him.

The smallest part of his most lovely hand
Finely taught our teacher,
A winged and lively bird,
Who gave an impromtu sermon,
Who taught us much
Of the Lord who is Master,
Of right measure, his power and wealth,
And wisdom, great and true.
Let us come to receive his learning,
Unmerited, from this learned bird:
Let the Lord be praised (by his own right),
Holy and pure, and no idol.
If our Lord is great, and great his praise
From just this one small part of earth,
Then what of the image of his greatness
Which comes from the whole of his fine work?
And through the image of the ascending steps
Of his gracious work, which he has made,
(Below and above the firmament,
Marvellously beyond number),
What of the greatness and pure loveliness,
Of God himself?

35 SELECTED VERSES FROM THE HYMNS
OF ANN GRIFFITHS

Ann Griffiths was born in 1776 and died soon after the birth of her first child, in 1805. Although lacking in formal education, she became one of the greatest hymn writers of Welsh revivalism. Her passionate and lyrical hymns combine perfect mastery of form — in the original — with a profound and personal reflection upon her faith. Welsh.

Wholly counter to my nature
Is the path ordained for me;
Yet I'll tread it, yes, and calmly
while thy precious face I see.

Pilgrim, faint and tempest-beaten,
lift thy gaze, behold and know
Christ the Lamb, our Mediator,
My sole pleasure, my sole comfort
Is thy glorious face to see.

His left hand, in heat of noon-day,
lovingly my head upholds.
And his right hand, filled with blessings,
tenderly my soul enfolds.

Thou thine all-excelling glory
Over all things dost display.
Let me drink for ever deeply
of salvation's mighty flood,
Till I thirst no more for ever
after any earthly good.

Thanks for ever,
and a hundred thousand thanks,
thanks while there is breath in me,
that there is an object to worship.

What more have I to do
with the base idols of earth?
O to abide
in his love all the days of my life.

O to have faith to look
with the angels above,
into the plan of salvation.

O to spend my whole life
sanctifying the holy name of God.

Medieval Religious Prose

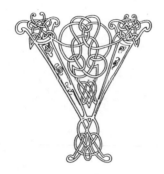

36 *from* 'ON THE CHRISTIAN LIFE'

Pelagius, who wrote this text, was either a British- or Irish-born monk of the fourth and fifth century who advocated views on grace and freedom which attracted the charge of heresy. He was accused of preaching that grace operated only externally, through Scripture and the teachings of the Church, and not within the human heart. His chief opponent was Augustine. Whatever views he may have held on grace, Pelagius advocated a strongly moral Christianity and exercised a stern critique of the half-hearted and fashionable Christianity of the late Roman world. The following extract is the opening passage to On the Christian Life *in which the author appears to acknowledge both his own humility and the humble nature of the rural and unsophisticated culture from which he comes. Latin.*

It is purely the occasion of your love (which I have grasped in heart and mind by God's power) and not faith in my own righteousness, nor the experience of wisdom, nor the glory of knowledge that has compelled me, a sinner first and last, more foolish than others and less experienced than all, to dare to write to you at length in order to counsel you to continue along the path of holiness and justice. And it is this too that so drives me and challenges me to speak, though I am sinful and ignorant, that even if I lack the knowledge to speak, still I may not remain silent. And so it is my desire and wish that you should be introduced to those whose wisdom is more abundant, whose eloquence is greater and knowledge fuller, whose conscience is freer from stain of sin, and who can rightly instruct you with words and examples. For not only has the darkness of foolishness and ignorance so blinded our mind that it can neither sense nor utter anything divine, but also conscience has con-victed it of all sins, so that even if our mind may have some light, still it conceals it. And so it is not only that we have nothing to say but also that we lack the confidence to offer what it is that we do have, since conscience prevents us. But you should nevertheless be content with our crude counsels, for as long as it seems wiser to you and better to do so, and consent to love. Do not weigh what he offers you, or inquire into what it is that he lacks; all that he has, he willingly shares. Do not look at the appearance of his gift so much as the intent of his soul, and note that he could have denied you all that he has and that he wishes to give you. He has offered you all that he can, and would have offered you what he does not have, had he been able to. And so they thirst, but too little, who cannot be content with the water of a shallow stream but must come to a purer and more abundant spring. Nor do I believe them to feel hunger enough who, when they have coarse bread, still wait for bread that is white and refined. And so you too, most beloved sister, who, I am sure, hunger and thirst immeasurably for the things of heaven: eat coarse bread for the moment, until you find bread of the whitest wheat, and drink the water of a shallow and muddy stream, until such time as you find one that is purer and more abundant. And do not for the moment disdain our bread, although it may seem rustic to you. For although rustic bread seems less refined, it is more substantial and more swiftly fills a hungry stomach, restoring strength to the weak, than white bread made from finely ground flour. I shall now give an account, to the best of my abilities, and an explanation, as far as I am able, of how a Christian should act. I can find no better preface to my treatise than first to discuss the very word 'Christian' and why it is that anyone should bear this name . . .

37 *from* 'TO A YOUNG MAN'

In this passage from his letter 'To a Young Man', we see Pelagius' frustration with the nominal Christian and a lukewarm Church. Latin.

First, then, get to know God's will, as contained in his law, so that you may be able to do it, since you can be certain that you are a true Christian only when you have taken the trouble to keep all God's commandments. I do not want you to pay any attention to the examples set by the majority, who claim the honour of belonging to this religion for themselves in name alone; for a prize so great belongs to only a few. How straight and narrow is the road that leads to life! And those who enter by it are few (Matthew 7.14). It is not the name but the deed which makes a Christian; you will find it harder to discover the essence of something than its title. For those who think they are Christians merely because they possess the name of 'Christian' are making a very serious mistake: they do not know that it is the name which belongs to the thing and not the thing to the name, and that it is right to call a man what he is but foolish to call him what he is not.

But perhaps you want to know what it means to be a Christian? A Christian is a man or woman in whom can be found these three attributes which all Christians should possess: knowledge, faith, obedience; knowledge by which we know God, faith by which we believe in him whom we know, obedience by which we render our allegiance and service to him in whom we believe.

38 *from 'TO CELANTIA'*

In the letter 'To Celantia', Pelagius stresses the moral and also deeply communitarian character of his ideal Christianity. Latin.

You should take out and write over your heart that sentence of the Gospel which is offered to us from the mouth of the Lord as the epitome of all righteousness: 'Whatever you wish that others should do to you, do also to them'; and to express the full force of this precept, he adds the statement: 'For this is the law and the prophets' (Matthew 7.12). The types and categories of righteousness are infinite, and it is most difficult not only to record them with the pen but also to grasp them in thought; but he includes them all in one brief sentence and either acquits or condemns the hidden consciences of men and women by the secret judgement of the mind.

With every act, therefore, with every word, even with every thought let this sentence be re-examined, since, like a mirror ready and always to hand, it reveals the nature of your will and also either exposes the wrong in the case of an unrighteous deed or shows cause for rejoicing in the case of a righteous one. For whenever you have the kind of attitude to another that you wish another to have towards you, then you are keeping to the way of righteousness; but whenever you are the kind of person to another that you want no one to be to you, you have abandoned the way of righteousness. See how demanding, how difficult is this whole business of keeping the divine law! See what it is that makes us protest against the Lord for giving us hard commands and say that we are being overwhelmed either by the difficulty or by the impracticability of these commands! Nor does it suffice that we do not carry out the commands without also pronouncing the one who gives them unfair, while we complain that the author of righteousness himself has imposed commands upon us which are not only difficult and arduous but even quite impossible. Whatever you wish, he says, that others would do to you, do also to them. He wants love between us to be established and maintained by mutual acts of kindness, and all to be united to one another by mutual love; so that, while each one provides for the other what all want provided for themselves, total righteousness, as in this commandment of God, may be the common benefit of humankind. And — how wonderful is God's mercy! how ineffable his kindness! — he promises us a reward if we love each other, that is, if we give to each other those things of which each one of us has need in return. But with a proud and ungrateful spirit, we oppose his will, when even his command is an act of kindness.

39 *from Cogitosus' LIFE OF BRIGID*

The following passages are taken from the Life of Brigid *by Cogitosus, which was written in the middle of the seventh century and is the earliest Life of an Irish saint. While Brigid of Kildare was almost certainly the foundress of a major monastic house in the late fifth or early sixth century, it is likely that imagery and themes associated with a powerful pre-Christian goddess figure became associated with her. In the passages which follow, the first is a classic instance of the Celtic saint's control over the elements, in this case fire and the power of the sun, while the final two show the particular interrelation between creatures and the Celtic saint, who appear to discover in each other the special presence of God.*

What I recount here is another episode which demonstrates her sanctity; one in which the action of her hand corresponded to the quality of her pure and virginal mind.

It happened that she was pasturing her sheep on a grassy spot on the plain when she was soaked by heavy rain, and she returned home in wet clothes. The sun shining through a gap in the building cast a ray which, at first glance, seemed to her to be a solid wooden beam fixed across the house. She placed her wet cloak upon it as if it were indeed solid, and the cloak hung securely from the incorporeal sunbeam. When the inhabitants of the house spread the word of this great miracle among the neighbours, they extolled the incomparable Brigid with fitting praise . . .

Once a solitary wild boar which was being hunted ran out from the woods, and in its headlong flight was brought suddenly into the herd of pigs that belonged to the most blessed Brigid. She noticed its arrival among her pigs and she blessed it. Thereupon it lost its fear and settled down among the herd. See how brute beasts and animals could oppose neither her bidding nor her wish, but served her tamely and humbly . . .

On another day the blessed Brigid felt a tenderness for some ducks that she saw swimming on the water and occasionally taking wing. She commanded them to come to her. A great flock of them flew on feathered wings towards her, without any fear, as if they were humans under obedience. When she had touched them with her hand and caressed them, she released them and let them fly into the sky. She praised the Creator of all things greatly, to whom all life is subject, and for the service of whom — as has already been said — all life is given . . .

40 *from the* LIFE OF MELANGELL

The version of the Life of Melangell *from which this translation was made is contained in a seventeenth century manuscript. Melangell (Latin: Monacella) is an important Welsh saint who was the foundress of Pennant Melangell in Montgomeryshire. Her feast day fell on May 27. Latin.*

In Powys there was once a certain most illustrious prince by the name of Brychwel Ysgithrog, who was the Earl of Chester and who at that time lived in the town of Pengwern Powys (which means in Latin the head of Powys marsh and is now known as Shrewsbury) and whose home or abode stood in that place where the college of St Chad is now situated. Now that very same noble prince gave his aforesaid home or mansion for the use of God as an act of almsgiving both by his own free will and from a sense of religious duty, making a perpetual grant of it for his own sake and for the sake of his heirs. When one day in the year of our Lord 604, the said prince had gone hunting to a certain place in Britain called Pennant, in the said principality of Powys, and when the hunting dogs of the same prince had started a hare, the dogs pursued the hare and he too gave chase until he came to a certain thicket of brambles, which was large and full of thorns. In this thicket he found a girl of beautiful appearance who, given up to divine contemplation, was praying with the greatest devotion, with the said hare lying boldly and fearlessly under the hem or fold of her garments, its face towards the dogs.

Then the prince cried 'Get it, hounds, get it!', but the more he shouted, urging them on, the further the dogs retreated and, howling, fled from the little animal. Finally, the prince, altogether astonished, asked the girl how long she had lived on her own on his lands, in such a lonely spot. In reply the girl said that she had not seen a human face for these fifteen years. Then he asked the girl who she was, her place of birth and origins, and in all humility she answered that she was the daughter of King Jowchel of Ireland and that 'because my father had intended me to be the wife of a certain great and generous Irishman, I fled from my native soil and with God leading me came here in order that I might serve God and the immaculate Virgin with my heart and pure body until my dying day'. Then the prince asked the girl her name. She replied that her name was Melangell. Then the prince, considering in his innermost heart the flourishing though solitary state of the girl, said: 'O most worthy virgin Melangell, I find that you are a handmaid of the true God and a most sincere follower of Christ. Therefore, because it has pleased the highest and all-powerful God to give refuge, for your merits, to this little wild hare with safe conduct and protection from the attack and pursuit of these savage and violent dogs, I give and present to you most willingly these my lands for the service of God, that they may be a perpetual asylum, refuge and defence, in honour of your name, excellent girl. Let neither king nor prince seek to be so rash or bold towards God that they presume to drag away any man or woman who has escaped here, desiring to enjoy protection in these your lands, as long as they in no way contaminate or pollute your sanctuary or asylum. But, on the other hand, if any wrongdoer who enjoys the protection of your sanctuary shall set out in any direction to do harm, then the free tenants known as abbots of your sanctuary, who alone know of their crimes, shall, if they find them guilty and culpable, ensure that they are released and handed over to the Powys authorities in order to be punished.'

This virgin Melangell, who was so very pleasing to God, led her solitary life, as stated above, for thirty-seven years in this very same place. And the hares, which are little wild creatures, surrounded her every day of her life, just as if they had been tame or domesticated animals, through which, by the aid of divine mercy, miracles and various other signs are not lacking for those who call upon her help and the grace of her favour with an inner motion of the heart.

After the death of the said most illustrious prince Brochwel, his son Tyssilio held the principality of Powys, followed by Conan, the brother of Tyssilio, Tambryd, Gurmylk and Durres the lame, all of whom sanctioned the said place of Pennant Melangell to be a perpetual sanctuary, refuge or safe haven for the oppressed (thereby confirming the acts of the said prince). The same virgin Melangell applied herself to establish and instruct certain virgins with all concern and care in the same region in order that they might persevere and live in a holy and modest manner in the love of God, and should dedicate their lives to divine duties, doing nothing else by day or by night. After this, as soon as Melangell herself had departed this life, a certain man called Elissa came to Pennant Melangell and wishing to debauch, violate and dishonour the same virgins, suddenly perished and died there in the most pitiful manner. Whoever has violated the above-mentioned liberty and sanctity of the said virgin has been rarely seen to escape divine vengeance on this account, as may be seen every day. Praises be to the most high God and to Melangell, his virgin.

41 *from the LIFE OF BEUNO*

The following extract is taken from the Life of Beuno, *which was perhaps written sometime during the twelfth century and was probably based on a Latin Life of this saint now lost. It is remarkable for containing a number of pagan motifs and for presenting the Christian saint essentially as a man of supernatural power. The second passage is interesting in that it links Beuno's lineage to Christ himself, rather in the manner of medieval Welsh genealogies of kings. Middle Welsh.*

One day Temic and his wife came to the church in order to hear Mass and Beuno's sermon, leaving his daughter behind to guard their home. She was the most beautiful girl in the world, and had not yet been given to a man. And as she remained on guard, she saw the king, who ruled that place, approaching her. His name was Caradoc. She rose up to greet him and was pleasant to him while the king, for his part, asked her where her father had gone. 'He went', she said, 'to the church. If you have any business with him, wait for him and he will soon be here.' 'I will not wait,' he said, 'unless you become my mistress.' The girl said: 'I am not fit to become your mistress since you are a great king and are from a line of kings. My blood is not noble enough for me to be your mistress. But wait here,' she said 'until I come from my room and I shall do what you desire.' Pretending to go to her room, she fled and made for the church where her father and mother were. The king saw her fleeing, and gave chase. As she reached the door of the church, he caught her up and struck off her head with his sword, which fell into the church while her body remained outside. Beuno, her mother and father saw what had happened, and Beuno stared into the face of the king and said: 'I ask God not to spare you and to respect you as little as you respected this good girl.' And in that moment the king melted away into a lake, and was seen no more in this world.

Then Beuno took the girl's head and placed it back with the body, covering the body with his cloak and saying to her mother and father who were mourning for her: 'Be quiet for a little while and leave her as she is until the Mass is over.' Then Beuno celebrated the sacrifice to God. When the Mass was finished, the girl rose up entirely healed and dried the sweat from her face; God and Beuno healed her. Where her blood fell to the earth, a spring was formed, which even today still heals people and animals from their illnesses and injuries. And that spring is called after the girl and is known as Ffynnon Wenfrewi. Many who had seen what had happened began to believe in Christ. One of those who believed was Cadfan, King of Gwynedd. He gave much land to Beuno . . .

And as Beuno's life was drawing to an end and his day approaching, on the seventh day after Easter he saw the heavens opening and the angels descending and ascending. Then Beuno said: 'I see the Trinity, the Father, the Son and the Holy Spirit, Peter and Paul and pure David, Deiniol, the saints and the prophets, the apostles and the martyrs appearing to me. And in the midst there I see seven angels standing before the throne of the highest Father and all the fathers of heaven, singing: "Blessed is the one you have chosen and have received and who shall dwell with you always." I hear the cry of the horn of the highest Father summoning me and saying to me: "My son, cast off your burden of flesh. The time is coming, and you are invited to share the feast that shall not end with your brothers. May your body remain in the earth while the armies of heaven and the angels bear your soul to the kingdom of heaven, which you have merited here through your works."

'This hour shall be the Day of Judgement when the Lord says to the saints: "Blessed sons of my Father, come to the kingdom that was prepared for you from the beginning of the world, where there shall be life without death, youth without old age and health without suffering, joy without grief, the saints in the highest rank with God the Father, in unity with the angels and archangels, in unity with the disciples of Jesus Christ, in unity with the nine grades of heaven, who did not sin, in the unity of the Father and the Son and the Holy Spirit, Amen."'

Let us too beseech the mercy of the all-powerful God by the help of St Beuno so that we may receive with him everlasting life in all eternity. Amen.

This is the line of Beuno. Beuno, son of Bugi, son of Gwynlliw, son of Tegid, son of Cadell Drynlluc, son of Categyrn, son of Gortheyrn, son of Gorthegyrn, son of Rhyddegyrn, son of Deheuwynt, son of Eudegan, son of Eudegern, son of Elud, son of Eudos, son of Eudoleu, son of Afallach, son of Amalech, son of Belim, son of Anna. The mother of that Anna was cousin to Mary the Virgin, the mother of Christ.

42 *from the LIFE OF DAVID*

This is the conclusion to the Life of David, *written in Latin by Rhigyfarch in around 1095. Although Rhigyfarch tells us that his work is based upon earlier manuscripts 'written in the manner of the elders', his work reflects the demands of a later and more sophisticated ecclesiastical establishment. This* Life of David *may well have been used to further the metropolitan claims of the see of St David in modern Pembrokeshire. In its final form it includes an account of the raising of David to the state of Archbishop and the claim that his successors inherit his primacy as spiritual leader of 'the entire British race'. Latin.*

Immediately after partaking of the Lord's Body and Blood, [David] was seized with pains and became ill. The service ended, he blessed the people and addressed everyone in these words: 'My brethren, persevere in those things which you have learned from me and have seen in me. On the third day, the first day of March, I shall go the way of my fathers. As for you, fare well in the Lord. I shall depart.' From that Sunday night until the fourth day after his death, all who had come remained weeping, fasting and keeping watch. Accordingly, when the third day arrived, the place was filled with choirs of angels, and was melodious with heavenly singing, and replete with the most delightful fragrance. At the hour of matins, while the monks were singing hymns, psalms and canticles, our Lord Jesus Christ deigned to bestow his presence for the consolation of the father [David], as he had promised by the angel. On seeing him, and entirely rejoicing in spirit, he said: 'Take me with you.' With these words, with Christ as his companion, he gave up his life to God, and, attended by the escort of angels, sought the gates of heaven. And so his body, borne on the arms of holy brethren, and accompanied by a great crowd, was committed to the earth with all honour and buried in the grounds of his own monastery; but his soul, set free from the bounds of this transitory life, is crowned throughout endless ages. Amen.

These and many other works the father did, while a mortal body weighed down the soul which it carried. We have provided only a few of the many examples that exist in order to satisfy the thirst of the ardent, by means of the vessel of my humble narrative. For, as one can never drain dry a river issuing forth from an everlasting spring with a narrow vessel of too limited capacity, so can no one commit to writing all the father's signs and miracles, his most devout practice of virtues and observance of precepts, even if he were to use a pen of iron. But as I have stated, these few I have gathered together as an example to all, and the father's glory, out of the very many that are scattered in the oldest manuscripts of our country, and chiefly of his own monastery. These, though eaten away along their edges and backs by the continuous gnawing of worms and the ravages of passing years, and written in the manner of the elders, have survived until now, and are gathered together and collected by me to the glory of the great father and for the benefit of others, that they shall not perish, as the bee sucks delicately with its mouth from the different blooms in a garden filled with flowers. And indeed, as for those works which, in the passing of time, he performs and has carried out more effectively since, having laid aside the burden of the flesh and having gazed upon the Deity face to face, he cleaves more closely to God, he who will may discover them through the witness of many. Moreover, as for myself, Rhigyfarch by name, who have somewhat rashly applied my slender mental abilities to this task, may those who read this work with a devout mind assist me with their prayers; so that, since the Father's mercy, like that of spring, has carried me through the summer heat of the flesh to the scanty flowering of my understanding, it may in the end, when the vapours of desire have vanished and before my course is ended, bring me the fruit of a good harvest through due and proper works. Then, when the tares of the enemy are separated, and the reapers shall have filled heaven's garners with purified sheaves, they may find a place for me, as a gleaning of the latest harvest, within the portals of the celestial gates, there endlessly to behold God, who is blessed above all things, for ever and ever. Amen.

43 *from the LIFE OF NINIAN*

The following is an extract from the Life of Ninian. *Ninian was a saint associated with the evangelization of the Picts and Britons of southern Scotland in the fourth and fifth centuries. He is said to have founded the 'white' or 'shining church' of Whithorn, dedicated to St Martin of Tours. This is a relatively late Life, although the passage given here can be paralleled with a number of other such accounts from the earlier Irish and Welsh hagiographical tradition.*

Wherever he went, he raised his soul to the things of heaven, either by prayer or contemplation. But whenever he rested from his journey, either for his own sake or for that of the animal he rode, he took out a book which he carried for the very purpose and liked to read or sing something, for he felt with the prophet: 'How sweet are your words in my throat, sweeter they are than honey in the mouth'. Therefore the divine power granted him such grace that even when resting in the open air, when reading in the heaviest rain, no dampness ever touched the book upon which his mind was concentrated. When everything around him was soaked, he sat alone with his little book in the downpour, as if protected by the roof of a house. Now it happened that when this most devout man was making a journey with one of his brothers (who was then still alive), also a very holy person by the name of Plebia, he rested from the fatigue of his journey, as was his custom, with the Psalms of David. And so, when they had gone some way, they left the road to rest and refreshed their souls with their psalters. But soon black clouds covered the clear sky, pouring back to earth those waters whch they had taken from it. What more can I say? The light air, like a room surrounding the servants of God, resisted the downpour like an impenetrable wall. But as they sang, the most blessed Ninian took his eyes from the book as an unlawful thought stirred in him and desire prompted by the devil. Immediately the rain fell upon him and his book, thus revealing what was hidden. Then the brother who was sitting beside him and who knew what had taken place, rebuked him gently, reminding him of his order and age and showing him how unseemly such things were in someone such as he. Straight away the man of God came to himself and blushing at having been overtaken by a vain thought, he banished it from his mind . . .

44 *from the PENITENTIAL OF CUMMEAN*

The Irish Penitential of Cummean *is the most comprehensive of the Celtic penitentials, and it makes use both of John Cassian's 'healing through opposites' principle and his eight cardinal sins. Its author was Cummaine Fota, Bishop of Clonfert, who died in 662. This penitential circulated widely on the*

Continent during the eighth and ninth centuries, and contributed, with other texts, to the adoption by the Catholic Church of the regular practice of private confession. Latin.

Here begins the prologue on the medicine for the salvation of souls.

1. As we are about to speak of the cure of wounds according to the precepts of the fathers before us, of sacred utterance to you, my most faithful brother, let us first indicate in a concise manner the medicines of Holy Scripture. 2. The first remission then is that by which we are baptized in water, according to this passage: 'Unless a man be born again of water and of the Holy Spirit, he cannot see the Kingdom of God'. 3. The second is the feeling of charity, as this text has it: 'Many sins are remitted unto her for she has loved much'. 4. The third is the fruit of almsgiving, according to this: 'As water quenches fire, so too do alms extinguish sin'. 5. The fourth is the shedding of tears, as the Lord says: 'Since Ahab wept in my sight and walked sad in my presence, I will not bring evil things in his days'. 6. The fifth is the confession of crimes, as the Psalmist testifies: 'I said, I will confess against myself my injustice to the Lord and you have forgiven the iniquity of my sin'. 7. The sixth is the affliction of heart and body, as the Apostle comforts us: 'I have given such a man to Satan for the destruction of his flesh, that his spirit may be saved in the day of our Lord Jesus Christ'. 8. The seventh is the amending of our ways, that is, the renunciation of vices, as the Gospel testifies: 'Now you are whole, sin no more, in case something worse happens to you'. 9. The eighth is the intercession of the saints, as this text states: 'If any be sick, let him bring the priests of the church and let them pray for him and lay their hands upon him, and anoint him with oil in the name of the Lord, and the prayer of faith shall save the sick man and the Lord shall raise him up, and if he be in sins, they shall be forgiven him,' and so forth, and: 'The continual prayer of a just man avails much before the Lord'. 10. The ninth is the reward of mercy and faith, as this says: 'Blessed are the merciful for they shall obtain mercy'. 11. The tenth is the conversion and salvation of others, as James assures us: 'He who causes a sinner to be converted from the error of his life shall save his soul from death and cover a multitude of sins'; but it is better for you, if you are weak, to lead a solitary life than to perish with many. 12. The eleventh is our pardon, as he that is the truth has promised, saying: 'Forgive and you shall be forgiven'.

13. The twelfth is the passion of martyrdom, as the one hope of our salvation then grants us pardon; and God replies to the cruel robber: 'Truly I say to you this day you shall be with me in Paradise'.

14. Therefore since these things are quoted on the authority of the Canon, it is right for you also to seek out the decrees of the fathers who were chosen by the mouth of the Lord, according to this passage: 'Ask your father and he will declare unto you, your elders and they will tell you'; indeed, 'Let the matter be referred to them'. And so they determine that the eight principal vices contrary to human salvation shall be healed by the eight remedies that are their contraries. For it is an old proverb: Contraries are cured by contraries. For he who without restraint commits what is forbidden ought to restrain himself even from what is permissible . . .

1. But this is to be carefully observed in all penance: the length of time anyone remains in his faults, what education he has received, with what passion he is assailed, with what courage he resists, with what intensity of weeping he seems to be afflicted, with what pressure he is driven to sin. 2. For almighty God, who knows the hearts of all and has made us all different, will not weigh the weight of sins in an equal scale of penance, as this prophecy says: 'For the gith shall not be threshed with saws, neither shall the cart wheel turn about upon the cummin; but the gith shall be beaten with a rod and the cummin with a staff, but bread corn shall be broken small' (Isaiah 28: 27–28), or as in this passage: 'The mighty shall be mightily tormented' (Wisdom 6.7). 3. For which reason a certain man, wise in the Lord, said: 'To whom more is entrusted, from him more shall be exacted' (cf. Luke 12.48). Thus the priests of the Lord who preside over the churches should learn that their share is given to them together with those whose faults they have caused to be forgiven. 4. What does it mean to cause a fault to be forgiven then unless, when you receive the sinner, by warning, exhortation, teaching and instruction you lead him to penance, correcting him from error, improving him from his vices, and making him such a person that God becomes favourable to him after his conversion, you are then said to cause his faults to be forgiven. 5. When you are a priest like this therefore, and this is your teaching and your word, there is given to you the share of those whom you have corrected, that their merit may be your reward and their salvation your glory.

Here ends this book written by Cummean.

45 *HOW THE MONK SHOULD PLEASE GOD*

This passage is taken from the third sermon of Columbanus and contains some of this great saint's reflections upon the monastic vocation. Columbanus, who was born in around 543, was the chief emissary of Irish monasticism on the Continent of Europe and was involved in the foundation of a number of important monastic sites there. Latin.

What is the best thing in the world? To please its Creator. What is his will? To fulfil what he commanded, that is, to live justly and devotedly to seek the eternal; for devotion and justice are the will of God who is himself devout and just. How do we reach this goal? By application. Then we must apply ourselves in devotion and justice. What helps to sustain this? Understanding which, while it winnows the remainder and finds nothing solid to remain in amongst those things which the world possesses, turns in wisdom to the one thing which is eternal. For the world will pass, and daily passes, and revolves towards its end (for what does it have to which it does not assign an end?) and somehow it is supported upon the pillars of vanity. But when vanity comes to an end, then it will fall and will not stand. But it cannot be said of the world that it shall not end. Thus by death and decline all things pass away and abide not. What then should the wise man love? A dull fiction, partly silent and partly sounding, which he sees and does not understand. For if he understood it, perhaps he would not love it, but it offends also in that it does not show itself as it is. For who understands, either in himself or another, being a flower of the earth and being earth from earth, by what deserving a child of God and citizen of heaven is made from what shall soon be earth and dust and from that which would never thrive without the help of the soul?

If anyone to whom God has granted it understands what life he should live in order to become eternal and not mortal, wise and not stupid, heavenly and not earthly, he should first keep his reason pure in order to use it for right living, and look not upon what is but upon what shall be. For that which is not shall be, and he should consider what he sees not by means of what he sees, and attempt to be what he was created and summon God's grace to assist his striving; for it is impossible for anyone to gain by his own efforts what he lost in Adam. But what help is it to gain discernment and not to use it well? He uses it well who lives in such a way that he need never repent but never forgets that he has repented, for a late repentance proves that we have had bad habits, while a good conscience commends our way of life. So what should a good discernment learn to love? Certainly that which makes it love all else besides, which always remains and never grows old. No other external thing should be loved, according to the reckoning of truth, except eternity and the eternal will, which is inspired and enlivened by the Eternal, Wonderful, Ineffable, Invisible, Incomprehensible, who fills all things and transcends all things, who is present to us and yet beyond our grasp.

46 *from Columbanus' 'SERMON THIRTEEN'*

An extract from a further sermon by Columbanus in which we see something of the mystical inspiration of early Irish monasticism. Latin.

Dearest brothers, do listen attentively to our words in the belief that you will hear something that needs to be heard, and refresh the thirst of your mind from the waters of the divine spring of which we now wish to speak. But do not quench that thirst; drink, but do not be filled. For now the living fountain, the fountain of life, calls us to himself and says: 'Let him who is thirsty come to me and drink.' And take note of what it is that you shall drink. Let Isaiah tell you, let the fountain himself tell you: 'But they have forsaken me the fountain of living water,' says the Lord. Thus the Lord himself, our God Jesus Christ, is the fountain of life, and so he calls us to himself, the fountain, that we may drink of him. He who loves drinks of him, he drinks who is filled with the word of God, who loves enough, who desires enough, he drinks who burns with the love of wisdom. Then let us Gentiles eagerly drink what the Jews have forsaken. For perhaps it was said of us with the Gentiles: 'He breaks off in amazement of mind, the heads of the mighty shall be moved, while they open not their jaws, like a poor man eating in secret'; and as if it were said of us also with all the perfect, of whom this was written, let us open the jaws of our inner man, as when eating that bread which came down from heaven, that we may eat hungrily and swiftly, in case anyone should see us, as if we ate in secret. Let us eat the same Lord Jesus Christ as bread, let us drink him as a fountain, who calls himself the 'living bread, who gives life to this world', as if to be eaten by us, and who likewise shows himself to be a fountain when he says: 'Let him who is thirsty come to me and drink', of which fountain the prophet also says: 'since with you is the fountain of life'.

Observe from where that fountain flows; for it comes from that place from where the bread also came down, since he is the same who is bread and fountain, the only Son, our God Christ the Lord, for whom we should always hunger. Although we eat him when we love him, though we feast on him when we desire him, let us still desire him like people who are ravenous. Likewise with the fountain, let us always drink of him with an overflowing love, let us always drink of him with a fullness of longing, and let the sweet savour of his loveliness ravish us. For the Lord is sweet and lovely; and although we eat and drink of him, let us still always hunger and thirst, since our food and drink can never be completely consumed, for though he is eaten, he is not eaten up, though he is drunk, he is not drained, since our bread is eternal and our fountain is everlasting, our fountain is sweet. Therefore the Prophet says: 'Go you who thirst to the fountain'; for that is the fountain of those who thirst, not of those who are replete, and so he calls to himself the hungry and the thirsty, whom he blessed elsewhere, who never have enough of drinking, but who thirst the more, the more they consume. We are right, my brothers, to desire the fountain of wisdom, the Word of God on high, to seek him, always to love him, in whom are hid, according to the Apostle's words, 'all the treasures of wisdom and knowledge', which he calls those who thirst to enjoy. If you thirst, drink the fountain of life; if you hunger, eat the bread of life, blessed are they who hunger for this bread and thirst for this fountain; though they are always eating and drinking, they still long to eat and drink. For that is lovely to excess which is always eaten and drunk, for which there is always a hunger and a thirst, always tasted and always desired. Therefore the Prophet-King says, 'taste and see how lovely, how pleasant is the Lord'. Therefore, my brothers, let us follow this calling, by which we are called to the fountain of life by the life who is the fountain, not only the fountain of living water, but also of eternal life, the fountain of light, indeed the fountain of glory; for from him come all these things, wisdom, life and eternal light. The Author of life is the fountain of life, the Creator of light, the fountain of glory. Therefore, spurning the things that are seen, journeying through the world, let us seek the fountain of glory, the fountain of life, the fountain of living water, in the upper regions of the heavens, like rational and most wise fishes, that there we may drink the living water which springs up to eternal life.

If only you would deign to admit me to that fountain, merciful God, righteous Lord, so that there I too might drink with your thirsting ones the living stream of the living fount of the living water and, ravished by his too great loveliness, might hold to him always on high and say: 'How lovely is the fount of living water, whose water does not fail, springing up to life eternal.' O Lord, you are yourself that fountain ever and again to be desired, although ever and again to be consumed. Give this water always, Lord Christ, that it may be in us too a fountain of water that lives and springs up to eternal life. I ask for great things; who does not know that. But you, King of Glory, know how to give great things and have promised great things. Nothing is greater than you yourself, and you have given yourself to us, you gave yourself for us. Therefore we ask that we may know what we love, for we ask for nothing other than that you should be given to us; for you are our all, our life, our light, our salvation, our food, our drink, our God. I ask that you inspire our hearts, our Jesus, with that breath of your Spirit, and wound our souls with your love, so that the soul of each one of us may be able to say in truth, 'show me him whom my soul has loved', for by love am I wounded. I desire that those wounds may be in me, O Lord. Blessed is such a soul which is thus wounded by love. Such a soul seeks the fountain, such a one drinks, but always thirsts when drinking, it always drinks when desiring, and always drinks when thirsting. Thus it always seeks by loving and is always healed by its wounding. And with this healing wound may our God and Lord Jesus Christ, that Physician of right-eousness and health, deign to wound the inward parts of our soul, who with the Father and the Holy Spirit is one for ever and ever. Amen.

47 AN OLD IRISH HOMILY

This sermon dates from around the ninth century and contains many of the themes of Celtic Christianity, including the giving of blessings, a concern with hell and judgement, and a truly cosmic sense of the meaning of religion which is visible in the listing of earthly analogues for heaven and hell. Later Old Irish.

We give thanks to almighty God, Lord of heaven and earth, for his mercy and forgiveness, for his love and his blessings which he has bestowed upon us in heaven and on earth. It is of him that the Prophet says: 'Confitentur tibi, Domine, omnia opera tua et sancti tui confiten-tur tibi'. For it is the duty of all the elements to give thanks to God and to bless him, as it is said: 'Benedicite omnia opera Domini Domino'. For God does not deny his present blessings even to sinners, as Scripture says: 'Bonus est Deus qui dat iustis et iniustis bona terrae in commune', that is, God is devoted and excellent who gives to the good and the evil the good things of the earth equally. For he is the one excellent God who is without beginning or end. He it is who has created all things, who has formed them and sustains them by the might of his power. He it is who nourishes and preserves and gladdens and illuminates and rules and has redeemed and renews all things. In him they trust; he it is for whom they wait, for he is King of kings and Lord of lords, Creator of heaven and earth, Maker of the angels, Teacher of the prophets, Master of the apostles, Giver of the Law, Judge of the men and women of the world. He is higher than the heavens, lower than the earth, wider than the seas.

It is our duty to give thanks to that Lord for his gifts. For the grateful soul who gives thanks to God for his grace is a temple and dwelling-place of God; as Peter says: 'Animam gratias agentem ac familiarem sibi facit deus'. That is, the man or woman who gives thanks to God for his blessings is an estate that belongs to the King of all. But they who are not grateful for the blessings of God are a temple and dwelling-place of the Devil; as Peter says: 'Ingratam animam malum possidet demon'. The evil demon possesses and inhabits the soul of the ungrateful who do not give thanks to God for his blessings. It is that thanksgiving which is meant when they say: 'Tibi gratias agunt animae nostrae pro innumeris beneficiis tuis'. That is, our souls give thanks to you, O Lord, for your blessings without number on heaven and earth.

And so may the blessing of the Lord of heaven and earth be on everyone with whom we have come into contact, on their possession of field and house, on their property both animate and inanimate, and on everyone who serves them and is obedient to them. May the earth give its fruits, may the air give its rainfall, may the sea give its fishes, may there be more grain and milk, more honey and wheat for everyone whose labour and goodwill we enjoy. May God give them a hundred-fold on this earth and the kingdom of heaven in the life to come. For they who receive Christ's people actually receive Christ, as he himself says: 'Qui vos recipit me recipit, qui vos spernit, me spernit'. That is, he who receives you, receives me, he who despises you, despises me.

But there are analogies to the kingdom of heaven and to hell in this world. First the analogy to hell, that is winter and snow, stormy weather and the cold, old age and decay, disease and death. The analogy to the kingdom of heaven however is summer and fair weather, flower and leaf, beauty and youth, feasts and feastings, prosperity and an abundance of every good thing.

But it is into hell that God shall cast sinners on Judgement Day, saying: 'Ite maledicti in ignem aeternum qui praeparatus est Diabolo et angelis eius', that is, 'Go, you cursed ones, into the everlasting fire which has been prepared for the Devil and his vile vassals'. Woe to them to whom the Lord shall say on the Day of Judgement that they shall dwell for ever in hell with its many and great torments. For its setting is deep, its surrounds are solid, its jaws are dark, its company are sorrowful, its stench is great, its monsters are everlasting, its earth is sunken, its surface is poisonous, it is an abyss to restrain, it is a prison to hold, it is a flame to burn, it is a net to hold fast, it is a scourge to lash, it is a blade to maim, it is a night to blind, it is smoke to suffocate, it is a cross to torture, it is a sword to punish.

In this way then these punishments are to be avoided: by hard work and study, by fasting and prayer, by righteousness and mercy, by faith and love. For whoever fulfils these commandments, God shall call them to himself on the Day of Judgement, saying to them: 'Venite benedicti patris mei, possidete regnum quod vobis paratum est ab origine mundi', which is 'Come, you blessed of my Father, possess the kingdom which has been prepared for you from the beginning of the world.'

We should strive then for the kingdom of heaven which is unlike the human dominion of the present world which earthly kings love. It blinds like mist, it slays like sleep, it wounds like a point, it destroys like a blade, it burns like fire, it drowns like a sea, it swallows like a pit, it devours like a monster. But not like that is the kingdom which the saints and the righteous strive for. It is a bright flower in its great purity, it is an open sea in its great beauty, it is a heaven full of candles in its true brilliance, it is the eye's delight in its great loveliness and pleasantness, it is a flame in its fairness, it is a harp in its melodiousness, it is a feast in its abundance of wine, it is a . . . in its true radiance. Blessed are they who shall come into the Kingdom where God himself is, a King, great, fair, powerful, strong, holy, pure, just, knowing, wise, merciful, loving, beneficent, old, young, wise, noble, glorious, without beginning, without end, without age, without decay. May we enter the kingdom of that King, may we merit it and may we dwell there *in saecula saeculorum*. Amen.

48 *from* 'THE EVERNEW TONGUE'

This is part of an apocryphal work possibly based on a lost Latin Apocalypse of Philip. 'Evernew Tongue' is the apostle Philip whose tongue has been cut out nine times and has been nine times miraculously restored. The text is essentially a dialogue between him and the Hebrew sages who are assembled on Mount Sion on Easter Eve, during which Philip explains to them the secrets of the creation. Of particular interest is the understanding of the cosmic significance of the resurrection since the body of Christ, like any other human body, contained within it all the elements of which the world is made. In the passage below, the two instances of angelic language are gibberish. Tenth or eleventh century. Old Irish with some Middle Irish forms.

Then suddenly, when it was the end of Easter Eve, something was heard: the sound in the clouds like the noise of thunder, or it was like the crash of an oak-tree bursting into flame. Meanwhile there was a thunderous blast, and suddenly a solar glow was seen like a radiant sun in the midst of the sound. That radiant solar glow turned round and round, so that eyesight could not comprehend it, for it was seven times more radiant than the sun.

Then suddenly something was heard, when the eyes of the company were expecting the sound; for they thought it was a sign of the Judgement. Something was heard: the clear voice that spoke in the language of angels: *Haeli habia felebe fae niteia temnibisse salis sal*, that is: 'Hear this story, you sons of men! I have been sent by God to speak with you'.

Then suddenly fainting and fear fell upon the hosts. Nor were they frightened without cause. The sound of the voice was like the shout of an army, except that it was clearer and plainer than the voices of human beings. It rang out over the multitude like the cry of a mighty wind, and yet was not louder than the conversation of friends in each other's ears; and it was sweeter than the melodies of the world.

The sages of the Hebrews answered and said: 'Tell us your name, your substance, your appearance.' Something was heard and the Ever-new Tongue spoke with an angelic voice: *Nathire uimbae o lebiae ua un nimbisse tiron tibia am biase sau fimblia febe ab le febia fuan*, that is: 'Truly, it was among the tribes of the earth that I was born; and by the conception of man and woman I was conceived. This is my name: Philip the Apostle. The Lord sent me to the tribes of the heathen to preach to them. Nine times my tongue has been cut out of my head and nine times I continued to preach again. Therefore my name among the people of heaven is the Evernew Tongue.'

The sages of the Hebrews said: 'Tell us what language it is that you speak to us.'

He said: 'There is a language of angels, and the language I speak to you is that of all the ranks of heaven. As for the beasts of the sea, reptiles, quadrupeds, birds, snakes and demons, they know it, and this is the language that all will speak at the Judgement.

'This then is what has driven me to you: to explain to you the wonderful tale which the Holy Spirit declared through Moses, son of Amram, of the creation of heaven and earth with all that exists in them. For it is of the making of heaven and earth that that tale speaks, and of the formation of the world, which was effected by Christ's resurrection from the dead on this eve of Easter. For every kind of matter, every element and every essence which is seen in the world were all combined in the body in which Christ arose, that is, in the body of every human being.

'In the first place there is the matter of wind and air. From this there came the afflation of breath in the human body. Then there is the matter of heat and boiling from fire. It is this that makes the red heat of blood in bodies. Then there is the matter of the sun and the other stars of heaven, and it is this that makes colour and light in the eyes of men and women. Then there is the matter of bitterness and saltness, and it is this that makes the bitterness of tears and the gall of the liver and the abundance of wrath in the hearts of men and women. Then there is the matter of the stones and of the clay of earth, and it is this that makes the mingling of flesh and bone and limbs in human beings. Then there is the matter of flowers and the beautiful hues of the earth, and it is this that makes the variegation and whiteness of faces and colour in the cheeks.

'All the world rose with him, for the essence of all the elements dwelt in the body which Jesus assumed. For if the Lord had not suffered on behalf of Adam's race, and if he had not risen after death, the whole world together with Adam's race would be destroyed on Judgement Day, and no creature of sea or land would be reborn, but the heavens, as far as the third heaven, would blaze. With the exception of only three of the high heavens, none would survive without being burned. There would be neither earth nor kindred, alive or dead, in the whole world, only hell and heaven, had the Lord not come to ransom them. All would have perished without renewal.

'For this,' says Philip, 'I have come to you, that I may make this known to you, for the fashioning of the world is obscure to you, as it has been recounted of old.'

49 *THE PRIEST AND THE BEES*

This story comes from the fifteenth century Liber Flavus Fergusiorum. *Middle Irish.*

There was a good, noble and reverend priest, who was God's own servant and bore the yoke of devotion to Christ. One day he went to tend a sick man, and as he was there, a swarm of bees came upon him. He had the sacred Host with him, and when he saw the swarm, he laid the sacred Host on the ground and gathered the swarm into his chest. He forgot the sacred Host lying there, and so went his way. And so it was that the bees went back again from him, and they found the Host and bore it away among them to the home where they lived. And they revered it lovingly, and made for it a lovely chapel of wax and an altar and a Mass chalice and a pair of priests, fashioning them finely of wax, to stand over the Host.

But as for the priest, he remembered the Host and went searching for it in anxiety and contrition, but could not find it anywhere. He was filled with sorrow and went to confession, and with the great contrition that seized him, he spent a whole year in penance. But an angel came to him at the end of the year and told him where the Host was, under reverent protection. And the angel told the priest to bring many people with him to see it. They went and saw it, and when they saw it, many of the people believed in it.

50 *from 'LETTER TO THE BELOVED WELSH'*

Morgan Llwyd (1619–1656) was a Welsh minister and author who, as a Puritan, fought with the Parliamentary forces during the Civil War. Towards the end of his life he read and translated the work of Jakob Böhme, and acquired from him an emphasis upon the presence of God within the human soul. The following extract was written in 1653.

Books are like springs of water, and for some today they are learned teachers who are like so many lights. And so, beloved Welshman, receive these few brief words in truth as an address to you in your own Welsh language.

Publishing many books is pointless; too many thoughts lead to fatigue; speaking many words is dangerous; playing host to many spirits is discomforting, and trying to answer all the reasonings of humankind is folly. But, dear reader, strive to know your own heart, and to enter through the narrow gate.

Many say no; few enter into life. Many dream, few awake; many loose their arrows, few strike their target; everyone speaks of God and gazes upon the work of his hands, but they do not see how near he is to them, giving breath to all and to us life of the spirit.

Almost everyone honours bats more than eagles, seeking to raise the human spirit above that of God, following their own lights without seeing the heavenly sun from the vantage point of the heights.

And, alas, how many Welshmen too, both wise and foolish, live in the sieve of vanity and in the gall of bitterness; they lie bound with untruth in the bed of Babel and feed their flesh in the devil's meadow, not knowing the invisible God who made them or the marvellous God who saved them, or the merciful God who cries out at their door to be let in and to make his dwelling in them.

But each one fumbles their way like a blindman along the wall and the borders looking (in their minds) for something to fill their eyes, to soften their hearts and to cool the burning desire within them, and they live as if on the edge of a shore, where the ebb and flow of flesh and blood ceaselessly beat upon them, who have no thought that they are poised on the edge of a precipice and the cliff of eternity, about to enter the world that shall last for ever, as they sleep beneath the paws of the cat of hell, murmering fondly in their slumber.

'If I had', says one, 'the native wit to know how the spinning wheel turns and to discover depths, then I would be happy and wise among people.'

Another says, 'If I were allowed to enjoy the origin of youth, even if I had to go through the hellish fire of adultery to find it, I would have what I wanted.' And another: 'If everyone were to bow to me as to God, then I would be a fine man.' A fourth says: 'If I had the bowels of the earth for my coffer, I would sleep easily and would be happy.' There is only the occasional one who enquires into the nature of the sun and moon and the appearance of the planets to his mind, and their orbits to his intelligence; but then an animal of a man says: 'If I had good food and strong drink and soft clothes, offspring and leisure and comfort, I would be content.' And the person whose mind is weary says: 'If I were in the grave, in the womb of my first mother, she would hold me and hide me from hell and the tribulation of life on earth.' That person is dreaming who says in their heart, 'If only I could be a scholar, a preacher, a doctor, a traveller, a soldier, a lawyer, a magistrate, or a treasurer, an aristocrat and a gentleman of character in my country, then I would be happier than ever before.'

But, O Welshman (I do not know your name though, by God's light, I know your nature), not one of these knows goodness, nor follows godliness, nor soars beyond the sun to the dweller in eternity, nor sees through faith the rock which produced it; but people try to live among the dead, seeking the sun in the pits of the earth, and you desire the rose, without wishing to come to the garden to fetch it, but die on your feet as you peep across the wall.

You are chasing the wind; you are eating the chaff. And the more you have of it, the more distress there is in your bowels and your mind; desire has deceived you and has imprisoned you in the chains of sin. You are eating grass with the animals, while the dew and power of the firmament rule you in the darkness and pride of Lucifer, who is the prince and root of evil angels, father of sin and torment. You knew neither yourself, poor thing, nor the one who made you, nor him who was sent to create you anew: Christ is the heart of God. If the Son were in your heart, he would destroy your sins, burn your desires, and fill your thoughts with wonderful light in heavenly love and unspeakable joy. Your soul is the image and likeness of God, and nothing can satisfy you but the fullness and image of the Highest, who is Son of the Father, Lamb of God, the First and the Last, the Source of Life, the Beauty of Angels, the Head of the Heavenly Ones, Root of the Universe, Centre of the Lights, Father of Spirits, the Word of God, the Craftsman who made Heaven and Earth, the Light of Men and Women, the Sun of the Scriptures, the Lover of Sinners, the Judge of Devils, the fifth King on the earth, the Ruler within God and humankind. He has one foot on the sea and the other on the shore. He obtains what he wills, and finishes what he begins, and no one can stop him.

He has filled the mind of God, and God is eternal mind, spirit both glorious and wonderful. He can fill your own mind too: he is always close to you, he sees you, hears you, tastes you, smells you, feels your presence everywhere day and night. But you are far from him; that is, you neither see nor hear him, and although he is constantly with you, you are not yet a companion to him. You cannot rest upon him, although he ever bears you in his arms, and though God listens to you at every moment, you have not yet succeeded in speaking a single word to him, in him and before him.

Although God takes care of you, filling your mouth with food, your body with life, your nostrils with air, your mind with reason, and your limbs with movement, you have not yet succeeded in conceiving of God in his Son, nor of his Son in his Spirit, nor of his Spirit in his word, nor of his word in your heart, nor of your heart within yourself, nor of yourself in this world, nor of this world in God, nor of God who is glorious in himself.

You should know that the universe which you see is like the bark of a tree, or a crust of bread, or a bone among dogs. It is the spirit or moistness within the creature which unites with your nature and causes desire in you, but beyond the life of nature within you your spirit walks and runs with the angels at all times. And beyond that within you there is the Blessed and Infinite Trinity, the Father, the Word and the Spirit (that is, will, delight and power, the three of these being one), and this far the human mind can penetrate through the spirit. But further than this and deeper there is the root and the ground in the immense, eternal and still unity that no eye can look upon and no mind grasp but his alone . . .

51 *from the WRITINGS OF HOWEL HARRIS*

Although he remained an Anglican, Howel Harris (1714–1773) was one of the most prominent leaders of the Methodist revival in eighteenth century Wales, which was strongly marked by a spirituality of pietism and mass conversion. In the first passage, which is taken from his diary, he speaks of his own conversion, while in the second, he gives spiritual advice to an acquaintance.

June 18th, 1735, being in secret prayer, I felt suddenly my heart melting within me like wax before the fire with love to God my Saviour; and I also felt not only love, peace, etc. but longing to be dissolved, and to be with Christ; then was a cry in my inmost soul, which I was totally unacquainted with before, Abba Father! Abba Father! I could not help calling God my Father; I knew that I was his child, and that he loved me, and heard me. My soul being filled and satiated, crying, 'Tis enough, I am satisfied. Give me strength, and I will follow thee through fire and water.' I could say I was happy indeed! There was in me a well of water, springing up to everlasting life, John 4.14. The love of God was shed abroad in my heart by the Holy Ghost, Romans 5.5 . . .

*

Rest not till you have the Spirit of God continually bearing witness with your spirit that you are born of God, till you can say I know on whom I have believed; — see that faith grows, and then love, meekness, brokenness of heart, godly sorrow, resignation of will, humility, holy fear, watchfulness, tenderness of conscience, and all other graces will grow, which are all destroyed by unbelief and doubts: — O beware of this hellish root, this hardens the heart, and alienates the soul from God. Still look up to Jesus, in him alone salvation is laid up, and can be conveyed to us by faith alone. — O glorious faith, when shall I hear thee preached up fully? All talking of holiness before faith is fruitless; but let us first lay the spring of it in our hearts, Christ living in us by faith, and the tree being once made good, the fruit will be so of course; and without this heart-purifying faith, this world-overcoming newborn creature of God, we may strive, and watch, and pray, but we shall be whited sepulchres at last. O see to the growth of this heavenly flower, and then all the wheels in your soul will keep a regular motion. Beware of false rests, and false peace. Rather, be wounded and mourning, till Christ speaks peace to your soul.

The Oral Tradition:
Gaelic Oral Literature
from Scotland and
Ireland

Carmina Gadelica: Hymns and Incantations

*With Illustrative Notes on Words, Rites, and
Customs, Dying and Obsolete: Orally Collected
in the Highlands and Islands of Scotland*

by Alexander Carmichael

INVOCATIONS

52 RUNE BEFORE PRAYER

Old people in the Isles sing this or some other short hymn before
prayer. Sometimes the hymn and the prayer are intoned in low
tremulous unmeasured cadences like the moving and moaning, the
soughing and the sighing, of the ever-murmuring sea on their own wild
shores.

They generally retire to a closet, to an out-house, to the lee of a knoll,
or to the shelter of a dell, that they may not be seen nor heard of men. I
have known men and women of eighty, ninety, and a hundred years of
age continue the practice of their lives in going from one to two miles to
the seashore to join their voices with the waves and their praises with
the praises of the ceaseless sea.

> I am bending my knee
> In the eye of the Father who created me,
> In the eye of the Son who purchased me,
> In the eye of the Spirit who cleansed me,
>   In friendship and affection.
> Through Thine own Anointed One, O God,
> Bestow upon us fullness in our need,
>   Love towards God,
>   The affection of God,
>   The smile of God,

The wisdom of God,
The grace of God,
The Fear of God,
And the will of God
To do on the world of the Three,
As angels and saints
Do in heaven;
Each shade and light,
Each day and night,
Each time in kindness,
Give Thou us Thy Spirit.

53 *GOD WITH ME LYING DOWN*

This poem was taken down in 1866 from Mary Macrae, Harris. She came from Kintail when young, with Alexander Macrae, whose mother was one of the celebrated daughters of Macleod of Rararsay, mentioned by Johnson and Boswell. Mary Macrae was rather under than over middle height, but strongly and symmetrically formed. She often walked with companions, after the work of the day was done, distances of ten and fifteen miles to a dance, and after dancing all night walked back again to the work of the morning fresh and vigorous as if nothing unusual had occurred. She was a faithful servant and an admirable worker, and danced at her leisure and carolled at her work like 'Fosgag Mhoire,' Our Lady's lark, above her.

The people of Harris had been greatly given to old lore and to the old ways of their fathers, reciting and singing, dancing and merry-making; but a reaction occurred, and Mary Macrae's old-world ways were abjured and condemned.

'The bigots of an iron time
Had called her simple art a crime.'

But Mary Macrae heeded not, and went on in her own way, singing her songs and ballads, intoning her hymns and incantations, and chanting her own 'port-a-bial,' mouth music, and dancing to her own shadow when nothing better was available.

I love to think of this brave kindly woman, with her strong Highland characteristics and her proud Highland spirit. She was a true type of a grand people gone never to return.

God with me lying down,
God with me rising up,
God with me in each ray of light,
Nor I a ray of joy without Him,
Nor one ray without Him.

Christ with me sleeping,
Christ with me waking,
Christ with me watching,
Every day and night,
Each day and night.

God with me protecting,
The Lord with me directing,
The Spirit with me strengthening,
For ever and for evermore,
Ever and evermore, Amen.
Chief of chiefs, Amen.

54 *THE INVOCATION OF THE GRACES*

Duncan Maclellan, crofter, Carnan, South Uist, heard this poem from Catherine Macaulay in the early years of his century. When the crofters along the east side of South Uist were removed, many of the more frail and aged left behind became houseless and homeless, moving among and existing upon the crofters left remaining along the west side of the island.

Among these was Catherine Macaulay. Her people went to Cape Breton. She came from Mol-a-deas, adjoining Corradale, where Prince Charlie lived for several weeks when hiding in South Uist after Culloden [in 1746]. Catherine Macaulay had seen the Prince several times, and had many reminiscences of him and of his movements among the people of the district, who entertained him to their best when much in need, and who shielded him to their utmost when sorely harassed.

Catherine Macaulay was greatly gifted in speaking, and was marvellously endowed with a memory for old tales and hymns, runes and incantations, and for unwritten literature and traditions of many kinds.

She wandered about from house to house, and from townland to townland, warmly welcomed and cordially received wherever she went, and remained in each place longer or shorter according to the population and the season, and as the people could spare the time to hear her. The description which Duncan Maclellan gave of Catherine Macaulay, and of the people who crowded his father's house to hear her night after night, and week after week, and of the discussions that followed her recitations, were realistic and instructive. Being then but a child he could not follow the meaning of this lore, but he thought many times since that much of it must have been about the wild beliefs and practices of his people of the long ago, and perhaps not so long ago either. Many of the poems and stories were long and weird, and he could only remember fragments, which came up to him as he lay awake, thinking of the present and the past, and of the contrast between the two, even in his own time.

I heard versions of this poem in other islands and in districts of the mainland, and in November 1888 John Gregorson Campbell, minister of Tiree, sent me a fragment taken down from Margaret Macdonald, Tiree. The poem must therefore have been widely known. In Tiree the poem was addressed to boys and girls, in Uist to young men and maidens. Probably it was composed to a maiden on her marriage. The phrase 'cala dhonn,' brown swan, would indicate that the girl was young — not yet a white swan.

> I bathe thy palms
> In showers of wine,
> In the lustral fire,
> In the seven elements,
> In the juice of the rasps,
> In the milk and honey,
> And I place the nine pure choice graces
> In thy fair fond face,
> > The grace of form,
> > The grace of voice,
> > The grace of fortune,
> > The grace of goodness,
> > The grace of wisdom,
> > The grace of charity,
> > The grace of choice maidenliness,
> > The grace of whole-souled loveliness,
> > The grace of godly speech.

Dark is yonder town,
Dark are those therein,
Thou art the brown swan,
Going in among them.
Their hearts are under thy control,
Their tongues are beneath thy sole,
Nor will they ever utter a word
  To give thee offence.

A shade art thou in the heat,
A shelter art thou in the cold,
Eyes art thou to the blind,
A staff art thou to the pilgrim,
An island art thou at sea,
A fortress art thou on land,
A well art thou in the desert,
  Health art thou to the ailing.

Thine is the skill of the Fairy Woman,
Thine is the virtue of Bride the calm,
Thine is the faith of Mary the mild,
Thine is the tact of the woman of Greece,
Thine is the beauty of Emir the lovely,
Thine is the tenderness of Darthula delightful,
Thine is the courage of Maebh the strong,
  Thine is the charm of Binne-bheul.

Thou art the joy of all joyous things,
Thou art the light of the beam of the sun,
Thou art the door of the chief of hospitality,
Thou art the surpassing star of guidance,
Thou art the step of the deer of the hill,
Thou art the step of the steed of the plain,
Thou art the grace of the swan of swimming,
  Thou art the loveliness of all lovely desires.

The lovely likeness of the Lord
Is in thy pure face,
The loveliest likeness that
Was upon earth.

The best hour of the day be thine,
The best day of the week be thine,
The best week of the year be thine,
The best year in the Son of God's domain be thine.

Peter has come and Paul has come,
James has come and John has come,
Muriel and Mary Virgin have come,
Uriel the all-beneficent has come,
Ariel the beauteousness of the young man has come,
Gabriel the seer of the Virgin has come,
Raphael the prince of the valiant has come,
And Michael the chief of the hosts has come,
    And Jesus Christ the mild has come,
    And the Spirit of true guidance has come,
    And the King of kings has come on the helm,
    To bestow on thee their affection and their love,
        To bestow on thee their affection and their love.

55 JESUS WHO OUGHT TO BE PRAISED

The reciter said that this poem was composed by a woman in Harris. She was afflicted with leprosy, and was removed from the community on the upland to dwell alone on the sea-shore, where she lived on the plants of the plains and on the shell-fish of the strand. The woman bathed herself in the liquid in which she had boiled the plants and shell-fish. All her sores became healed and her flesh became new — probably as the result of the action of the plants and shell-fish.

Leprosy was common everywhere in mediaeval times. In Shetland the disease continued till towards the end of the last century. Communities erected lazar-houses to safeguard themselves from persons afflicted with leprosy. Liberton, now a suburb of Edinburgh, derives its name from a lazaretto having been established there.

The shrine of St James of Compostello in Spain was famous for the cure of leprosy. Crowds of leper pilgrims from the whole of Christendom resorted to this shrine, and many of them were healed to the glory of the Saint and the enrichment of his shrine. In their gratitude, pilgrims offered costly oblations of silks and satins, of raiments and vestments, of silver and gold, of pearls and precious stones, till the shrine of St James of Compostello became famous throughout the world. The bay of Compostello was famed for fish and shell-fish, and the leper pilgrims who came to pray at the altar of the Saint and to bestow gifts at his shrine were fed on those and were healed — according to the belief of the period, by the miraculous intervention of the Saint. As the palm was the badge of the pilgrims to Jerusalem, the scallop-shell was the badge of the pilgrims to Compostello: 'My sandal shoon and scallop-shell'.

> It were as easy for Jesu
> To renew the withered tree
> As to wither the new
> Were it His will so to do.
> > Jesu! Jesu! Jesu!
> > Jesu! meet it were to praise Him.

> There is no plant in the ground
> But is full of His virtue,
> There is no form in the strand
> But is full of His blessing.
> > Jesu! Jesu! Jesu!
> > Jesu! meet it were to praise Him.

> There is no life in the sea,
> There is no creature in the river,
> There is naught in the firmament,
> But proclaims His goodness.
> > Jesu! Jesu! Jesu!
> > Jesu! meet it were to praise Him.

> There is no bird on the wing,
> There is no star in the sky,
> There is nothing beneath the sun,
> But proclaims His goodness.
> > Jesu! Jesu! Jesu!
> > Jesu! meet it were to praise Him.

56 *THE GUARDIAN ANGEL*

Thou angel of God who hast charge of me
From the dear Father of mercifulness,
The shepherding kind of the fold of the saints
To make round about me this night;

Drive from me every temptation and danger,
Surround me on the sea of unrighteousness,
And in the narrows, crooks and straits,
Keep thou my coracle, keep it always.

Be thou a bright flame before me,
Be thou a guiding star above me,
Be thou a smooth path below me,
And be a kindly shepherd behind me,
To-day, to-night, and for ever.

I am tired and I a stranger,
Lead thou me to the land of angels;
For me it is time to go home
To the court of Christ, to the peace of heaven.

57 *DESIRES*

May I speak each day according to Thy justice,
Each day may I show Thy chastening, O God;
May I speak each day according to Thy wisdom,
Each day and night may I be at peace with Thee.

Each day may I count the causes of Thy mercy,
May I each day give heed to Thy laws;
Each day may I compose to Thee a song,
May I harp each day Thy praise, O God.

May I each day give love to Thee, Jesu,
Each night may I do the same;
Each day and night, dark and light,
May I laud Thy goodness to me, O God.

58 *INVOCATION FOR JUSTICE*

The administration of law and justice throughout the Highlands and
Islands before the abolition of heritable jurisdictions was inadequate —
men being too often appointed to administer justice not from their
fitness but from their influence. Probably the feeling of distrust engendered by this absence of even-handed justice evoked these poems from
the consciousness of the people and led them to appeal their cause to a
Higher Court.

The litigant went at morning dawn to a place where three streams
met. And as the rising sun gilded the mountain crests, the man placed
his two palms edgeways together and filled them with water from the
junction of the streams. Dipping his face into this improvised basin, he
fervently repeated the prayer, after which he made his way to the court,
feeling strong in the justice of his cause. On entering the court and
looking round the room, the applicant for justice mentally, sometimes
in an undertone, said —

> God sain the house
> From site to summit;
> My word above every person,
> The word of every person below my foot.

The ceremonies observed in saying these prayers for justice, like
those observed on many similar occasions, are symbolic. The bathing
represents purification; the junction of three streams, the union of the
Three Persons of the Godhead; and the spreading rays of the morning
sun, divine grace. The deer is symbolic of wariness, the horse of
strength, the serpent of wisdom, and the king of dignity.

> I will wash my face
> In the nine rays of the sun,
> As Mary washed her Son
>   In the rich fermented milk.

> Love be in my countenance,
> Benevolence in my mind,
> Dew of honey in my tongue,
>   My breath as the incense.

Black is yonder town,
Black are those therein,
I am the white swan,
    Queen above them.

I will travel in the name of God,
In likeness of deer, in likeness of horse,
In likeness of serpent, in likeness of king:
    Stronger will it be with me than with all persons.

59 SLEEP BLESSING

The night prayers of the people are numerous. They are called by various names, as: 'Beannachadh Beinge' — Bench-Blessing, 'Beannachadh Bobhstair' — Bolster Blessing, 'Beannachadh Cluasaig' — Pillow Blessing, 'Beannachadh Cuaiche' — Couch Blessing, 'Coich Chuaiche' — Couch Shrining, 'Altachadh Cadail' — Sleep Prayer; and other terms. Many of these prayers are become mere fragments and phrases, supplemented by the people according to their wants and wishes at the time.

It is touching and instructive to hear these simple old men and women in their lowly homes addressing, as they say themselves, 'Dia mor nan dul, Athair nan uile bheo,' the great God of life, the Father of all living. They press upon Him their needs and their desires fully and familiarly, but with all the awe and deference due to the Great Chief whom they wish to approach and attract, and whose forgiveness and aid they would secure. And all this in language so homely yet so eloquent, so simple yet so dignified, that the impressiveness could not be greater in proudest fane.

60 SLEEP CONSECRATION

I lie down to-night
With fair Mary and with her Son,
With pure-white Michael,
And with Bride beneath her mantle.

I lie down with God,
And God will lie down with me,
I will not lie down with Satan,
Nor shall Satan lie down with me.

O God of the poor,
Help me this night,
Omit me not entirely
From thy treasure-house.

For the many wounds
That I inflicted on Thee,
I cannot this night
Enumerate them.

Thou King of the blood of Truth,
Do not forget me in Thy dwelling-place,
Do not exact from me for my transgressions,
Do not omit me in Thine ingathering.
       In Thine ingathering.

61 *THE SOUL-SHRINE*

The Soul-Shrine is sung by the people as they retire to rest. They say that the angels of heaven guard them in sleep and shield them from harm. Should any untoward event occur to themselves or to their flocks, they avow that the cause was the deadness of their hearts, the coldness of their faith, and the fewness of their prayers.

God, give charge to Thy blessed angels,
    To keep guard around this stead to-night,
A band sacred, strong, and steadfast,
    That will shield this soul-shrine from harm.

Safeguard Thou, God, this household to-night,
    Themselves and their means and their fame,
Deliver them from death, from distress, from harm,
    From the fruits of envy and of enmity.

Give Thou to us, O God of peace,
Thankfulness despite our loss,
To obey Thy statutes here below,
And to enjoy Thyself above.

62 *A RESTING PRAYER*

God shield the house, the fire, the kine,
Every one who dwells herein to-night.
Shield myself and my beloved group,
Preserve us from violence and from harm;
Preserve us from foes this night,
For the sake of the Son of the Mary Mother,
In this place, and in every place wherein they dwell to-night,
On this night and on every night,
This night and every night.

63 *THE BAPTISM BLESSING*

It is known that a form of baptism prevailed among the Celts previous to the introduction of Christianity, as forms of baptism prevail among pagan people now. Whenever possible the Celtic Church chris-tianized existing ceremonies and days of special observance, grafting the new on the old, as at a later day Augustine did in southern Britain. Immediately after its birth the nurse or other person present drops three drops of water on the forehead of the child. The first drop is in the name of the Father, representing wisdom; the second drop is in the name of the Son, representing peace; the third drop is in the name of the Spirit, representing purity. If the child be a male the name 'Maol-domhnuich,' if a female the name 'Griadach,' is applied to it temporarily. 'Maol-domhnuich' means tonsured of the Lord, and 'Griadach' is rendered Gertrude. When the child is ecclesiastically baptized — generally at the end of eight days — the temporary is super-seded by the permanent name. This lay baptism is recognized by the Presbyterians, the Anglican, the Latin, and the Greek Churches. If the child were not thus baptized it would need to be carefully guarded lest the fairies should spirit it away before the ecclesiastical baptism took place, when their power over it ceased. The lay baptism also ensured that in the event of death the child should be buried in consecrated ground.

Thou Being who inhabitest the heights
Imprint Thy blessing betimes,
Remember Thou the child of my body,
In Name of the Father of peace;
When the priest of the King
On him puts the water of meaning,
Grant him the blessing of the Three
Who fill the heights.
The blessing of the Three
Who fill the heights.

Sprinkle down upon him Thy grace,
Give Thou to him virtue and growth,
Give Thou to him strength and guidance,
Give Thou to him flocks and possessions,
Sense and reason void of guile,
Angel wisdom in his day,
That he may stand without reproach
In Thy presence.
He may stand without reproach
In Thy presence.

64 *THE SOUL LEADING*

Death blessings vary in words but not in spirit. These death blessings are known by various names, as: 'Beannachadh Bais,' Death Blessing, 'Treoraich Anama,' Soul Leading, 'Fois Anama,' Soul Peace, and other names familiar to the people.

The soul peace is intoned, not necessarily by a cleric, over the dying, and the man or the woman who says it is called 'anam-chara,' soul-friend. He or she is held on special affection by the friends of the dying person ever after. The soul peace is slowly sung — all present earnestly joining the soul-friend in beseeching the Three Persons of the God-head and all the saints of heaven to receive the departing soul of earth. During the prayer the soul-friend makes the sign of the cross with the right thumb over the lips of the dying.

The scene is touching and striking in the extreme, and the man or woman is not to be envied who could witness unmoved the distress of these lovable people of the West taking leave of those who are near and dear to them in their pilgrimage, as they say, of crossing 'abhuinn dubh a bhais' — the black river of death; 'cuan mor na duibhre' — the great ocean of darkness; and 'beanntaibh na bith-bhuantachd' — the mountains of eternity. The scene may be a lowly cot begrimed with smoke and black with age, but the heart is not less warm, the tear is not less bitter, and the parting is not less distressful, than in the court of the noble or in the palace of royalty . . .

When a person gives up the ghost the soul is seen ascending like a bright ball of light into the clouds. Then it is said: —

> The poor soul is now set free
> Outside the soul-shrine;
> O kindly Christ of the free blessings,
> Encompass Thou my love in time . . .

65 THE DEATH BLESSING

God, omit not this woman from Thy covenant,
And the many evils which she in the body committed,
That she cannot this night enumerate.
> The many evils that she in the body committed,
> That she cannot this night enumerate.

Be this soul on Thine own arm, O Christ,
Thou King of the City of Heaven,
And since Thine it was, O Christ, to buy the soul,
At the time of the balancing of the beam,
At the time of the bringing of judgement,
Be it now on Thine own right hand,
> Oh! on Thine own right hand.

And be the holy Michael, king of angels,
Coming to meet the soul,
And leading it home
To the heaven of the Son of God.
> The Holy Michael, high king of angels,

Coming to meet the soul,
And leading it home
To the heaven of the Son of God.

66 *THE NEW MOON*

This little prayer is said by old men and women in the islands of Barra.
When they first see the new moon they make their obeisance to it as to a
great chief. The women curtsey gracefully and the men bow low,
raising their bonnets reverently. The bow of the men is peculiar,
partaking somewhat of the curtsey of the women, the left knee being
bent and the right drawn forward towards the middle of the left leg in a
curious but not inelegant manner.

The fragment of moon-worship is now a matter of custom rather
than of belief, although it exists over the whole British Isles.

In Cornwall the people nod to the new moon and turn silver in their
pockets. In Edinburgh cultured men and women turn the rings on their
fingers and make their wishes. A young English lady told the writer that
she had always been in the habit of bowing to the new moon, till she had
been bribed out of it by her father, a clergyman, putting money in her
pocket lest her lunar worship should compromise him with his bishop.
She naively confessed, however, that among the free mountains of Loch
Etive she reverted to the good customs of her fathers, from which she
derived great satisfaction!

In name of the Holy Spirit of grace,
In name of the Father of the City of peace,
In name of Jesus who took death off us,
Oh, in name of the Three who shield us in every need,
If well thou hast found us to-night,
Seven times better mayest thou leave us without harm,
        Thou bright white Moon of the seasons,
        Bright white Moon of the seasons.

67 *AUGURY OF MARY*

The 'frith,' augury, was a species of divination enabling the 'frithir,'
augurer, to see into the unseen. This divination was made to ascertain

the position and condition of the absent and the lost, and was applied to man and beast. The augury was made on the first Monday of the quarter and immediately before sunrise. The augurer, fasting, and with bare feet, bare head, and closed eyes, went to the doorstep and placed a hand on each jamb. Mentally beseeching the God of the unseen to show him his quest and to grant him his augury, the augurer opened his eyes and looked steadfastly straight in front of him. From the nature and position of the objects within his sight, he drew his conclusions.

Many men in the Highlands and Islands were famed augurers, and many stories, realistic, romantic, and extremely curious, are still told of their divinations.

The people say that the Virgin made an augury when Christ was missing, and that it was by means of this augury that Mary and Joseph ascertained that Christ was in the Temple disputing with the doctors. Hence this divination is called 'frith Mhoire,' — the augury of Mary; and 'frithircachd Mhoire,' — the auguration of Mary.

The 'frith' of the Celt is akin to the 'frett' of the Norsemen. Probably the surnames Freer, Frere, are modifications of 'frithir,' augurer. Persons bearing this name claim that their progenitors were astrologers to the kings of Scotland.

> God over me, God under me,
> God before me, God behind me,
> I on Thy path, O God,
> > Thou, O God, in my steps.

> The augury made of Mary to her Son,
> The offering made of Bride through her palm,
> Sawest Thou it, King of life? —
> > Said the King of life that He saw.

> The augury made by Mary for her own offspring,
> When He was for a space amissing,
> Knowledge of truth, not knowledge of falsehood,
> > That I shall truly see all my quest.

> Son of beauteous Mary, King of life,
> Give Thou me eyes to see all my quest,
> With grace that shall never fail, before me,
> > That shall never quench nor dim.

68 *OMENS*

The people believed in omens of birds and beasts, fishes and insects, and of men and women. These omens were innumerable, and a few only can be mentioned.

The fisher would deem it a bad omen to meet a red-haired woman when on his way to fish; and were the woman defective in mind or body, probably the man would return home muttering strong adjectives beneath his breath. On the other hand, it was lucky for a girl to find the red hair of a woman in the nest of certain birds, particularly in the nest of the wheatear . . .

69 *OMENS*

I heard the cuckoo with no food in my stomach,
I heard the stock-dove on the top of the tree,
I heard the sweet singer in the copse beyond,
And I heard the screech of the owl of the night.

I saw the lamb with his back to me,
I saw the snail on the bare flag-stone,
I saw the foal with his rump to me,
I saw the wheatear on a dyke of holes,
I saw the snipe while sitting bent,
And I forsaw that the year would not
      Go well with me.

SEASONS

70 *THE GENEALOGY OF BRIDE*

The Genealogy of Bride was current among people who had a latent belief in its efficacy. Other hymns to Bride were sung on her festival, but nothing now remains except the name and fragments of the words. The names are curious and suggestive, as: 'Ora Bhride,' Prayer of Bride, 'Lorg Bhride,' Staff of Bride, 'Luireach Bhride,' Lorica of Bride, 'Lorig

Bhride,' Mantle of Bride, 'Brot Bhride,' Corslet of Bride, and others. La Feill Bhride, St Bridget's Day, is the first of February, new style, or the thirteenth according to the old style, which is still much in use in the Highlands. It was a day of great rejoicing and jubilation in olden times, and gave rise to innumerable sayings, as —

Feast of the Bride, feast of the maiden.

Melodious Bride of the fair palms.

Thou Bride fair charming,
Pleasant to me the breath of thy mouth,
When I would go among strangers
Thou thyself wert the hearer of my tale.

There are many legends and customs connected with Bride. Some of these seem inconsistent with one another, and with the character of the Saint of Kildare. These seeming inconsistencies arise from the fact that there were several Brides, Christian and pre-Christian, whose person-alities have become confused in the course of centuries — the attributes of all being now popularly ascribed to one. Bride is said to preside over fire, over art, over all beauty, 'fo cheabhar agus fo chuan,' beneath the sky and beneath the sea. And man being the highest type of ideal beauty, Bride presides at his birth and dedicated him to the Trinity. She is the Mary and the Juno of the Gael. She is much spoken of in connection with Mary — generally in relation to the birth of Christ. She was the aid-woman of the Mother of Nazareth in the lowly stable, and she is the aid-woman of the mothers of Uist in their humble homes.

It is said that Bride was the daughter of poor pious parents, and the serving-maid in the inn of Bethlehem. Great drought occurred in the land, and the master of the hostel went away with his cart to procure water from afar, leaving with Bride, 'faircil buirn agus breacag arain,' a stoup of water and a bannock of bread to sustain her till his return. The man left injunctions with Bride not to give food or drink to any one, as he had left only enough for herself, and not to give shelter to any one against his return.

As Bride was working in the house two strangers came to the door. The man was old, with brown hair and grey beard, and the woman was young and beautiful, with oval face, straight nose, blue eyes, red lips, small ears, and golden brown hair, which fell below her waist. They asked the serving-maid for a place to rest, for they were footsore and weary, for food to satisfy their hunger, and for water to quench their thirst. Bride could not give them shelter, but she gave them of her own bannock and of her own stoup of water, of which they partook at the door; and having thanked Bride the strangers went their way, while Bride gazed wistfully and sorrowfully after them. She saw that the sickness of life was on the young woman of the lovely face, and her heart was sore that she had not in her power to give them shade from the heat of the sun, and cover from the cold of the dew. When Bride returned into the house in the darkening of the twilight, what was stranger to her to see than that the bannock of bread was whole, and the stoup of water full, as they had been before! She did not know under the land of the world what she would say or what she would do. The food and the water of which she herself had given them, and had seen them partake, without a bit or a drop lacking from them! When she recovered from her wonderment Bride went out to look after the two who had gone their way, but she could see no more of them. But she saw a brilliant golden light over the stable door, and knowing that it was not a 'dreag a bhais,' a meteor of death, she went into the stable and was in time to aid and minister to the Virgin Mother, and to receive the Child into her arms, for the strangers were Joseph and Mary, and the child was Jesus Christ, the Son of God, come to earth, and born in the stable of the hostel of Bethlehem. . . . When the Child was born Bride put three drops of water from the spring of pure water on the tablet of His forehead, in the name of God, in the name of Jesus, in the name of the Spirit. When the master of the inn was returning home, and ascending the hill on which his house stood, he heard the murmuring music of a stream flowing past his house, and he saw the light of a bright star above his stable door. He knew from these signs that the Messiah was come and that Christ was born . . . for it was in the seership of the people that Jesus Christ, the Son of God, would be born in Bethlehem, the town of David. And the man rejoiced with exceeding joy at the fulfilment of the prophecy, and he went to the stable and worshipped the new Christ, whose infant cradle was the manger of the horses.

Thus Bride is called 'ban-chuideachaidh Moire,' the aid-woman of Mary. In this connection, and in consequence thereof, she is called 'Muime Chriosda,' foster-mother of Christ; 'Bana-ghoistidh Mhic De,' the god-mother of the Son of God; 'Bana-ghoistidh Iosda Criosda nam bann agus nam beannachd,' god-mother of Jesus Christ of the bindings and blessings. Christ again is called 'Dalta Bride,' the foster-son of

Bride; 'Dalta Bride bith nam beannachd,' the foster-son of Bride of the blessings; 'Daltan Bride,' little fosterling of Bride, a term of endearment.

John the beloved is called 'Dalta Moire,' foster-son of Mary, and 'Comhdhalta Chriosda,' the foster-brother, literally co-foster, of Christ. Fostership among the Highlanders was a peculiarly close and tender tie, more close and more tender even than blood. There are many proverbs on the subject, as '. . . blood to the twentieth, fostership to the hundredth degree'. A church in Islay is called 'Cill Daltain,' the Church of the Fosterling.

When a woman is in labour, the midwife or the woman next to her in importance goes to the door of the house, and standing on the 'fadbuinn,' sole-sod, door-step, with her hands on the jambs, softly beseeches Bride to come:

> Bride! Bride! come in,
> Thy welcome is truly made,
> Give thou relief to the woman,
> And give the conception to the Trinity.

When things go well, it indicates that Bride is present and is friendly to the family; and when they go ill, that she is absent and offended. Following the action of Bride at the birth of Christ, the aid-woman dedicates the child to the Trinity by letting three drops of clear cold water fall on the tablet of his forehead.

The aid-woman was held in reverence by all nations. Juno was worshipped with greater honour than any other deity of ancient Rome, and the Pharaohs paid tribute to the aid-women of Egypt. . . .

On Bride's Eve the girls of the townland fashion a sheaf of corn into the likeness of a woman. They dress and deck the figure with shining shells, sparkling crystals, primroses, snowdrops, and any greenery they may obtain. In the mild climate of the Outer Hebrides several species of plants continue in flower during winter, unless the season be exceptionally severe. The gales of March are there the destoyers of plant-life. A specially bright shell or crystal is placed over the heart of the figure. This is called 'reul-iuil Bride,' the guiding star of Bride, and typifies the star over the stable door of Bethlehem, which led Bride to the infant Christ. The girls call the figure 'Bride,' 'Brideag,' Bride, Little Bride, and carry it in procession, singing the song of 'Bride bhoidheach oigh nam mile beus,' Beauteous Bride, virgin of a thousand charms. The 'banal Bride,' Bride maiden band, are clad in white, and have their hair down, symbolising purity and youth. They visit every house, and every person is expected to give a gift to Bride and to make obeisance to her. The gift may be a shell, a spar, a crystal, a flower, or a bit of greenery to decorate the person of Bride. Mothers, however, give 'bonnach Bride,' a Bride bannock, 'cabag Bride,' a Bride cheese, or 'rolag Bride,' a Bride roll of butter. Having made the round of the place the girls go to a house to make the 'feis Bride,' Bride feast. They bar the door and secure the windows of the house, and set Bride where she may see and be seen by all. Presently the young men of the community come humbly asking permission to honour Bride. After some parleying they are admitted and make obeisance to her.

Much dancing and singing, fun and frolic, are indulged in by the young men and maidens during the night. As the grey dawn of the Day of Bride breaks they form a circle and sing the hymn of 'Bride bhoidheach muime chorr Chriosda,' Beauteous Bride, choice foster-mother of Christ. They then distribute 'fuidheal na feisde,' the frag-ments of the feast — practically the whole, for they have partaken very sparingly, in order to have the more to give — among the poor women of the place.

A similar practice prevails in Ireland. There the churn staff, not the corn sheaf, is fashioned into the form of a woman, and is called 'Brideog,' little Bride. The girls come clad in their best, and the girl who has the prettiest dress gives it to Brideog. An ornament something like a Maltese cross is affixed to the breast of the figure. The ornament is composed of straw, beautifully and artistically interlaced by the deft fingers of the maidens of Bride. It is called 'rionnag Brideog', the star of little Bride. Pins, needles, bits of stone, bits of straw, and other things are given to Bride as gifts, and food by the mothers.

Customs assume the complexion of their surroundings, as fishes, birds, and beasts assimilate the colours of their habitats. The seas of the 'Garbh Chriocha,' Rough Bounds in which the cult of Bride has longest lived, abound in beautiful iridescent shells, and the mountains in bright sparkling stones, and they are utilised to adorn the ikon of Bride. In other districts where the figure of Bride is made, there are no shining shells, no brilliant crystals, and the girls decorate the image with artistically interlaced straw.

The older women are also busy on the Eve of Bride, and the great preparations are made to celebrate her Day, which is the first day of spring. They make an oblong basket in the shape of a cradle, which they call 'leaba Bride,' the bed of Bride. It is embellished with much care. They take a choice sheaf of corn, generally oats, and fashion it into the form of a woman. They deck this ikon with gay ribbons from the loom, sparkling shells from the sea, and bright stones from the hill. All the sunny sheltered valleys around are searched for primroses, daisies, and other flowers that open their eyes in the morning of the year. This lay figure is called Bride, 'dealbh Bride,' the ikon of Bride. When it is dressed and decorated with all the tenderness and loving care the women can lavish upon it, one woman goes to the door of the house, and standing on the step with her hands on the jambs, calls softly into the darkness, 'Tha leaba Bride deiseal,' Bride's bed is ready. To this a ready woman behind replies, 'Thigeadh Bride steach, is e beatha Bride,' Let Bride come in, Bride is welcome. The woman at the door again addresses Bride, . . . Bride, come thou in, thy bed is made. Preserve the house for the Trinity. The women then place the ikon of Bride with great ceremony in the bed they have so carefully prepared for it. They place a small straight white wand (the bark being peeled off) beside the figure. This wand is variously called 'slatag Bride,' the little rod of Bride, 'slachdan Bride,' the little wand of Bride, and 'barrag Bride,' the birch of Bride. The wand is generally of birch, broom, bramble, white willow, or other sacred wood, 'crossed' or banned wood being carefully avoided. A similar rod was given to the kings of Ireland at their coronation, and to the Lords of the Isles at their installment. It was straight to typify justice, and white to signify peace and purity — bloodshed was not to be needlessly caused. The women then level the ashes on the hearth, smoothing and dusting them over carefully. Occasionally the ashes, surrounded by a roll of cloth, arc placcd on a board to safeguard them against disturbance from draughts or other contingencies. In the early morning the family closely scan the ashes. If they find the marks of the wand of Bride they rejoice, but if they find 'lorg Bride,' the footprint of Bride, their joy is very great, for this is a sign that Bride was present with them during the night, and is favour-able to them and that there is increase in a family, in flock, and in field during the coming year. Should there be no marks on the ashes, and no trace of Bride's presence, the family are dejected. It is to them a sign that she is offended, and will not hear their call. To propitiate her and gain her ear the family offer oblations and burn incense. The oblation generally is a cockerel, some say a pullet, buried alive near the junction of three streams, and the incense is burnt on the hearth when the family retire for the night.

In the Highlands and Islands St Bride's Day was called 'La Cath Choileach,' Day of Cock-fighting. The boys brought cocks to the school to fight. The most successful cock was called 'coileach buadha,' victor cock, and its proud owner was elected king of the school for the year. A defeated bird was called 'fuidse,' craven, 'coileach fuidse,' craven cock. All the defeated, maimed, and killed cocks were the perquisites of the schoolmaster. In the Lowlands, 'La Coinnle,' Candlemas Day, was the day thus observed.

It is said in Ireland that Bride walked before Mary with a lighted candle in each hand when she went up to the Temple for purification. The winds were strong on the Temple heights, and the tapers were unprotected, yet they did not flicker nor fall. From this incident Bride is called 'Bride boillsge,' Bride of brightness. This day is occasionally called 'La Fheill Bride nan Coinnle,' the Feast Day of Bride of the Candles, but more generally 'La Fheill Moire nan Coinnle,' the Feast Day of Mary of the Candles — Candlemas Day.

The serpent is supposed to emerge from its hollow among the hills on St Bride's Day, and a propitiatory hymn was sung to it. Only one verse of this hymn has been obtained, apparently the first. It differs in different localities: —

> Early on Bride's morn
> The serpent shall come from the hole,
> I will not molest the serpent,
> Nor will the serpent molest me.

Other versions say: —

> The Feast Day of the Bride,
> The daughter of Ivor shall come from the knoll,
> I will not touch the daughter of Ivor,
> Nor shall she harm me.

*

> On the Feast Day of Bride,
> The head will come off the 'caiteanach,'
> The daughter of Ivor will come from the knoll
> With tuneful whistling.

*

> The serpent will come from the hole
> On the brown Day of Bride,
> Though there should be three feet of snow
> On the flat surface of the ground.

The 'daughter of Ivor' is the serpent; and it is said that the serpent will not sting a descendant of Ivor, he having made 'tabhar agus tuis,' offering and incense, to it, thereby securing immunity from its sting for himself and his seed for ever.

> On the day of Bride of the white hills
> The noble queen will come from the knoll,
> I will not molest the noble queen,
> Nor will the noble queen molest me.

These lines would seem to point to serpent-worship. One of the most curious customs of Bride's Day was the pounding of the serpent in effigy. The following scene was described to the writer by one who was present: —

I was one of several guests in the hospitable house of Mr John Tolmie of Uignis, Skye. One of my fellow guests was Mrs Macleod, widow of Major Macleod of Stein, and daughter of Flora Macdonald. Mrs Macleod was known among her friends as 'Major Ann'. She combined the warmest of hearts with the sternest of manners, and was the admiration of old and young for her wit, wisdom, and generosity. When told that her son had fallen in a duel with the celebrated Glengarry — the Ivor MacIvor of Waverley — *she exclaimed, '. . . Good thou art my son! good thou art my son! thou the white love of thine own mother! Better the hero's death than the craven's life; the brave dies but once, the coward many times.' In a company of noblemen and gentlemen at Dunvegan Castle, Mrs Macleod, then in her 88th year, danced the reel of Tullock and other reels, jigs, and strathspays as lightly as a girl in her teens. Wherever she was, all strove to show Mrs Macleod attention and to express the honour in which she was held. She accepted all these honours and attentions with grace and dignity, and without any trace of vanity or self-consciousness. One morning at breakfast at Uignis some one remarked that this was the Day of Bride. 'The Day of Bride,' repeated Mrs Macleod meditatively, and with a dignified bow of apology rose from the table. All watched her movements with eager curiosity. Mrs Macleod went to the fireside and took up the tongs and a bit of peat and walked out to the doorstep. She then took off her stocking and put the peat into it, and pounded it with the tongs. And as she pounded the peat on the step, she intoned a 'rann,' rune, only one verse of which I can remember:*

> *This is the day of Bride,*
> *The Queen will come from the mound,*
> *I will not touch the queen,*
> *Nor will the queen touch me.*

Having pounded the peat and replaced her stocking, Mrs Macleod returned to the table, apologising for her remissness in not remembering the Day earlier in the morning. I could not make out whether Mrs Macleod was serious or acting, for she was a consummate actress and the delight of young and old. Many curious ceremonies and traditions in connection with Bride were told that morning but I do not remember them.

The pounding in the stocking of the peat representing the serpent would indicate destruction rather than worship, perhaps the bruising of the serpent's head. Probably, however, the ceremony is older, and designed to symbolise something now lost.

Gaelic lore is full of sayings about serpents. These indicate close observation, 'Tha cluas nathrach aige,' — he has the ear of a serpent (he hears keenly but does not speak); 'Tha a bhana-bhuitseach lubach mar an nathair,' — the witch-woman is crooked as a serpent; 'Is e an t-iorball is neo-chronail dhiot, cleas na nathrach nimhe,' — the tail is the least harmful of thee, the trick of the serpent venomous.

> Though smooth be thy skin,
> Venomous is the sting of thy mouth;
> Thou art like the dun serpent,
> Take thine own road.

> The beauteous woman, ungenerous,
> And she full of warm words,
> Is like the brindled serpent,
> And the sting of greed is in her.

[. . .]

In Barra, lots are cast for the 'iolachan iasgaich,' fishing-banks, on Bride's Day. These fishing banks of the sea are as well known and as accurately defined by the fishermen of Barra as are the qualities and boundaries of their crofts on land, and they apportion them with equal care. Having ascertained among themselves the number of boats going to the long-line fishing, the people divide the banks accordingly. All go to church on St Bride's Day. After reciting the virtues and blessings of Bride, and the examples to be drawn from her life, the priest reminds his hearers that the great God who made the land and all thereon, also made the sea and all therein, and that . . . the wealth of the sea and the plenty of the land, the treasury of Columba and the treasury of Mary, are His gift to them that follow Him and call upon His name, on rocky hill or on crested wave. The priest urges upon them to avoid disputes and quarrels over their fishing, to remember the poor, the widow and the orphan, now left to the fatherhood of God and to the care of His people. Having come out of church, the men cast lots for the fishing-banks at the church door. After this, they disperse to their homes, all talking loudly and discussing their luck or unluck in the drawing of the lots. A stranger would be apt to think that the people were quarrelling. But it is not so. The simultaneous talking is their habit, and the loudness of their speaking is the necessity of their living among the noise of winds and waves, whether on sea or on shore. Like the people of St Kilda, the people of Barra are warmly attached to one another, the joy of one and the grief of another being the joy and grief of all.

The same practice of casting lots for their fishing-banks prevails among the fisher-folks of the Lofodin Islands, Norway.

From these traditional observations, it will be seen that Bride and her services are near to the hearts and lives of the people. In some phases of her character she is much more to them than Mary is.

Dedications to Bride are common throughout Great Britain and Ireland.

GENEALOGY OF BRIDE

> The genealogy of the holy maiden Bride,
> Radiant flame of gold, noble foster-mother of Christ.
> Bride the daugher of Dugall the brown,
> Son of Aodh, son of Art, son of Conn,
> Son of Crearar, son of Cis, son of Carmac, son of Carruin.

Every day and every night
That I say the genealogy of Bride,
I shall not be killed, I shall not be harried,
I shall not be put in cell, I shall not be wounded,
Neither shall Christ leave me in forgetfulness.

No fire, no sun, no moon shall burn me,
No lake, no water, nor sea shall drown me,
No arrow or fairy dart of fay shall wound me,
And I under the protection of my Holy Mary,
And my gentle foster-mother is my beloved Bride.

71 *BRIDE THE AID-WOMAN*

There came to me assistance,
Mary fair and Bride;
As Anna bore Mary,
As Mary bore Christ,
As Eile bore John the Baptist
Without flaw in him,
Aid thou me in mine unbearing,
  Aid me O Bride!

As Christ was conceived of Mary
Full perfect on every hand,
Assist thou me, foster-mother,
The conception to bring from the bone;
And as thou didst aid the Virgin of joy,
Without gold, without corn, without kine,
Aid thou me, great is my sickness,
  Aid me, O Bride!

72 *THE BELTANE BLESSING*

Bealltain, Beltane, is the first day of May. On May Day all the fires of the district were extinguished and 'tein eigin,' need-fire, produced on the knoll. This fire was divided in two, and people and cattle rushed through for purification and safeguarding against 'ealtraigh agus dosgaidh,' mischance and murrain, during the year. The people obtained fires for their homes from this need-fire. The practice of producing the need-fire came down in the Highlands and Islands to the first quarter of this century. The writer found traces of it in such distant places as Arran, Uist, and Sutherland. In 1895 a woman in Arran said that in the time of her father the people made the need-fire on the knoll, and then rushed home and brought out their 'creatairean,' creatures, and put them round the fire to safeguard them, 'bho 'n bhana bhuitsich mhoir Nic-creafain,' from the arch-witch Crawford.

The ordeal of passing through the fires gave rise to a proverb which I heard used by an old man in Lewis in 1873:— . . . Ah Mary! sonnie, it were worse for me to do that for thee, than to pass between the two great fires of Beall. . . .

73 *THE BELTANE BLESSING*

Mary, thou mother of saints,
Bless our flocks and bearing kine;
Hate nor scath nor let come near us,
Drive from us the ways of the wicked.

Keep thine eye every Monday and Tuesday
On the bearing kine and the pairing queys;
Accompany us from hill to sea,
Gather thyself the sheep and their progeny.

Every Wednesday and Thursday be with them,
Be thy gracious hand always about them;
Tend the cows down to their stalls,
Tend the sheep down to their folds!

Every Friday be thou, O Saint, at their head,
Lead the sheep from the face of the bens,
With their innocent little lambs following them,
Encompass them with God's encompassing.

Every Saturday be likewise with them,
Bring the goats in with their young,
Every kid and goat to the sea side,

And from the Rock of Aegir on high,
With cresses green about its summit.

The strength of the Triune be our shield in distress,
The strength of Christ, His peace and His Pasch,
The strength of the Spirit, Physician of health,
And of the precious Father, the King of grace.

[. . .]

And of every other saint who succeeded them
And who earned the repose of the kingdom of God.

Bless ourselves and our children,
Bless every one who shall come from our loins,
Bless him whose name we bear,
Bless, O God, her from whose womb we came.

Every holiness, blessing and power,
Be yielded to us every time and every hour,
In name of the Holy Threefold above,
Father, Son, and Spirit everlasting.

Be the Cross of Christ to shield us downward,
Be the Cross of Christ to shield us upward,
Be the Cross of Christ to shield us roundward,
Accepting our Beltane blessing from us,
        Accepting our Beltane blessing from us.

74 *THE FEAST DAY OF MARY*

The Feast Day of Mary the Great is the 15th day of August. Early in the
morning of this day the people go into their fields and pluck ears of
corn, generally bere, to make the 'Moilean Moire.' These ears are laid
on a rock exposed to the sun, to dry. When dry, they are husked in the
hand, winnowed in a fan, ground in a quern, kneaded on a sheep-skin,
and formed into a bannock, which is called 'Moilean Moire,' the fatling
of Mary. The bannock is toasted before a fire of fagots of rowan, or
some other sacred wood. Then the husbandman breaks the bannock

and gives a bit to his wife and to each of his children, in order according to their ages, and the family raise the 'Iolach Mhoire Mhathar,' the Paean of Mary Mother who promised to shield them, and who did and will shield them from scath till the day of death. While singing thus, the family walk sunwide round the fire, the father leading, the mother following, and the children following according to age.

After going round the fire, the man puts the embers of the faggot-fire, with bits of old iron, into a pot, which he carries sunwise round the outside of his house, sometimes round his steadings and his fields, and his flocks gathered in for the purpose. He is followed without as within by his household, all singing the praise of Mary Mother the while.

The scene is striking and picturesque, the family being arrayed in their brightest and singing their best.

> On the feast day of Mary the fragrant,
> Mother of the Shepherd of the flocks,
> I cut me a handful of the new corn,
> I dried it gently in the sun,
> I rubbed it sharply from the husk
>   With mine own palms.
>
> I ground it in a quern on Friday,
> I baked it on a fan of sheep-skin,
> I toasted it to a fire of rowan,
> And I shared it round my people.
>
> I went sunways round my dwelling,
> In the name of the Mary Mother,
> Who promised to preserve me,
> Who did preserve me,
> And who will preserve me,
> In peace, in flocks,
> In righteousness of heart,
> In labour, in love,
> In wisdom, in mercy,
> For the sake of Thy Passion.
> Thou Christ of grace
> Who till the day of my death
> Wilt never forsake me!
>   Oh, till the day of my death
>   Wilt never forsake me!

75 *MICHAEL, THE VICTORIOUS*

St Michael is spoken of as 'brian Michael,' god Michael.

> Thou wert the warrior of courage
> Going on the journey of prophecy,
> Thou wouldst not travel on a cripple,
> Thou didst take the steed of the god Michael,
> He was without bit in his mouth,
> Thou didst ride him on the wing,
> Thou didst leap over the knowledge of Nature.

St Michael is the Neptune of the Gael. He is the patron saint of the sea, and of maritime lands, of boats and boatmen, of horses and horsemen thoughout the West. As patron saint of the sea St Michael had temples dedicated to him round the coast wherever Celts were situated. Examples of these are Mount St Michael in Brittany and in Cornwall, and Aird Michael in South and in North Uist, and elsewhere. Probably Milton had this phase of St Michael's character in view. As patron saint of the land St Michael is represented riding a milk-white steed, a three-pronged spear in his right hand and a three-cornered shield in his left. The shield is inscribed 'Quis ut Deus,' a literal translation of the Hebrew Mi-cha-el. Britannia is substituted for the archangel on sea and St George on land.

On the 29th September a festival in honour of St Michael is held throughout the Western Coasts and Isles. This is much the most imposing pageant and much the most popular demonstration of the Celtic year. Many causes conduce to this — causes which move the minds and hearts of the people to their utmost tension. To the young the Day is a day of promise, to the old a day of fulfilment, to the aged a day of retrospect. It is a day when pagan cult and Christian doctrine meet and mingle like the lights and shadows on their own Highland hills.

The Eve of St Michael is the eve of bringing in the carrots, of baking the 'struan,' of killing the lamb, of stealing the horses. The Day of St Michael is the Day of the early mass, the day of the sacrificial lamb, the day of the oblation 'struan,' the day of the distribution of the lamb, the day of the distribution of the 'struan,' the day of pilgrimage to the burial-ground of their fathers, the day of the burial-ground service, the day of the burial-ground circuiting, the day of giving and receiving the carrots with wishes and acknowledgements, and the day of the 'oda' — the athletics of the men and the racing of the horses. And the Night of Michael is the night of the dance and the song, of the merry-making, of the love-making, and of the love-gifts. . . .

As may be seen from some of the poems, the duty of conveying the souls of the good to the abode of bliss is assigned to Michael. When the soul has parted from the body and is being weighed, the archangel of heaven and the archangel of hell preside at the beam, the former watching that the latter does not put . . . claw of hand nor talon of foot near the beam. Michael and all the archangels and angels of heaven sing songs of joy when the good in the soul outweighs the bad, while the devil howls as he retreats.

MICHAEL, THE VICTORIOUS

Thou Michael the victorious,
I make my circuit under thy shield,
Thou Michael of the white steed,
And of the bright brilliant blades,
Conqueror of the dragon,
Be thou at my back,
Thou ranger of the heavens,
Thou warrior of the King of all,
O Michael the victorious,
My pride and my guide,
O Michael the victorious,
The glory of mine eye.

I make my circuit
In the fellowship of my saint,
On the machair, on the meadow,
On the cold heathery hill;
Though I should travel ocean
And the hard globe of the world
No harm can e'er befall me
'Neath the shelter of thy shield;
O Michael the victorious,
Jewel of my heart,
O Michael the victorious,
God's shepherd thou art.

Be the sacred Three of Glory
Aye at peace with me,
With my horses, with my cattle,
With my woolly sheep in flocks.
With the crops growing in the field
Or ripening in the sheaf,
On the machair, on the moor,
In cole, in heap, or stack.
> Every thing on high or low,
> Every furnishing and flock,
> Belong to the holy Triune of glory,
> And to Michael the victorious.

LABOUR

76 *BLESSING OF THE KINDLING*

The kindling of the fire is a work full of interest to the housewife. When 'lifting' the fire in the morning the woman prays, in an undertone, that the fire may be blessed to her and to her household, and to the glory of God who gave it. The people look upon fire as a miracle of Divine power provided for their good — to warm their bodies when they are cold, to cook their food when they are hungry, and to remind them that they too, like the fire, need constant renewal mentally and physically.

I will kindle my fire this morning
In presence of the holy angels of heaven,
In presence of Ariel of the loveliest form,
In presence of Uriel of the myriad charms,
Without malice, without jealousy, without envy,
Without fear, without terror of any one under the sun,
But the Holy Son of God to shield me.
> Without malice, without jealousy, without envy,
> Without fear, without terror of any one under the sun,
> But the Holy Son of God to shield me.

God, kindle Thou in my heart within
A flame of love to my neighbour,

To my foe, to my friend, to my kindred all,
To the brave, to the knave, to the thrall,
O Son of the loveliest Mary,
From the lowliest thing that liveth,
To the Name that is highest of all.
      O Son of the loveliest Mary,
      From the lowliest thing that liveth,
      To the Name that is highest of all.

77 *SMOORING THE FIRE*

Peat is the fuel of the Highlands and Islands. Where wood is not obtainable the fire is kept in during the night. The process by which this is accomplished is called in Gaelic smaladh; in Scottish, smooring; and in English, smothering, or more correctly, subduing. The ceremony of smooring the fire is artistic and symbolic, and is performed with loving care. The embers are evenly spread on the hearth — which is generally in the middle of the floor — and formed into a circle. This circle is then divided into three equal sections, a small boss being left in the middle. A peat is laid between each section, each peat touching the boss, which forms a common centre. The first peat is laid down in the name of the God of Life, the second in the name of the God of Peace, the third in the name of the God of Grace. The circle is then covered over with ashes sufficient to subdue but not to extinguish the fire, in the name of the Three of Light. The heap slightly raised in the centre is called 'Tula nan Tri', the Hearth of the Three. When the smooring operation is complete the woman closes her eyes, stretches her hand, and softly intones one of the many formulae current for these occasions.

Another way of keeping embers for morning use is to place them in a pit at night. The pit consists of a hole in the clay floor, generally under the dresser. The pit may be from half a foot to a foot in depth and diameter, with a flag fixed in the floor over the top. In the centre of this flag there is a hole by which the embers are put in and taken out. Another flag covers the hole to extinguish the fire at night, and to guard against accidents during the day. This extinguishing fire-pit is called 'slochd guail', coke or coal-pit. This coke or charcoal is serviceable in kindling the fire.

The sacred Three
To save,
To shield,
To surround
The hearth,
The house,
The household,
This eve,
This night,
Oh! this eve,
This night,
And every night,
Each single night.
                    Amen.

78 *THE QUERN BLESSING*

The quern songs, like all the labour songs of the people, were composed in a measure suited to the special labour involved. The measure changed to suit the rhythmic motion of the body at work, at times slow, at times fast, as occasion required. I first saw the quern at work in October 1860 in the house of a cottar at Fearann-an-leatha, Skye. The cottar woman procured some oats in the sheaf. Roughly evening the heads, and holding the corn over an old partially-dressed sheep-skin, she switched off the grain. This is called 'gradanadh,' quickness, from the expert handling required in the operation. The whole straw of the sheaf was not burnt, only that part of the straw to which the grain was attached, the flame being kept from proceeding further. The straw was tied up and used for other purposes.

Having fanned the grain and swept the floor, the woman spread out the sheep-skin again and placed the quern thereon. She then sat down to grind, filling and relieving the quern with one hand and turning it with the other, singing the while to the accompaniment of the 'whirr! whirr! whirr! birr! birr! birr!' of the revolving stone. Several strong sturdy boys in scant kilts, and sweet comely girls in nondescript frocks, sat round the peat fire enjoying it fully, and watching the work and listening to the song of their radiant mother. . . .

When the mills were erected the authorities destroyed the querns in order to compel the people to go the mills and pay multure, mill dues.

This wholesale and inconsiderate destruction of querns everywhere entailed untold hardships on thousands of people living in roadless districts and in distant isles without mills, especially during storms. Among other expedients to which the more remote people resorted was the searching of ancient ruins for the 'pollagan,' mortar mills, of former generations. The mortar is a still more primitive instrument for preparing corn than the quern. . . .

   The quern and mortar are still used in outlying districts of Scotland and Ireland, though isolatedly and sparingly.

THE QUERN BLESSING

On Ash Eve
We shall have flesh,
We should have that
We should have that.

The cheek of hen,
Two bits of barley,
That were enough
That were enough.

We shall have mead,
We shall have spruce,
We shall have wine,
We shall have feast.
We shall have sweetness and milk produce,
Honey and milk,
Wholesome ambrosia,
Abundance of that,
Abundance of that.

We shall have harp,
We shall have harp,
We shall have lute,
We shall have horn.
We shall have sweet psaltery
Of the melodious strings
And the regal lyre,
Of the songs we shall have,
Of the songs we shall have.

The calm fair Bride will be with us,
The gentle Mary mother will be with us.
Michael the chief
Of glancing glaves,
And the King of kings
And Jesus Christ,
And the Spirit of peace
And of grace will be with us,
Of grace will be with us.

79 *MILKING CROON*

The milking songs of the people are numerous and varied. They are sung to pretty airs, to please the cows and to induce them to give their milk. The cows become accustomed to these lilts and will not give their milk without them, nor, occasionally, without their favourite airs being sung to them. The fondness of Highland cows for music induces owners of large herds to secure milkmaids possessed of good voices and some 'go'. It is interesting and animating to see three or four comely girls among a fold of sixty, eighty, or a hundred picturesque Highland cows on meadow or mountain slope. The moaning and heaving of the sea afar, the swish of the wave on the shore, the carolling of the lark in the sky, the unbroken song of the mavis on the rock, the broken melody of the merle in the brake, the lowing of the kine without, the response of the calves within the fold, the singing of the milkmaids in unison with the movement of their hands, and of the soft sound of the snowy milk falling into the pail, the gilding of hill and dale, the glowing of the distant ocean beyond, as the sun sinks into the sea of golden glory, constitute a scene which the observer would not, if he could, forget.

Come, Brendan, from the ocean,
Come, Ternan, most potent of men,
Come, Michael valiant, down
And propitiate to me the cow of my joy.
Ho my heifer, ho heifer of my love,
Ho my heifer, ho heifer of my love.
My beloved heifer, choice cow of every shieling,
For the sake of the High King take to thy calf.

Come, beloved Colum of the fold,
Come, great Bride of the flocks,
Come, fair Mary from the cloud,
And propitiate to me the cow of my love.
　　Ho my heifer, ho heifer of my love.

The stock-dove will come from the wood,
The tusk will come from the wave,
The fox will come but not with wiles,
To hail my cow of virtues.
　　Ho my heifer, ho heifer of my love.

80 *HUNTING BLESSING*

A young man was consecrated before he went out to hunt. Oil was put on his head, a bow was placed in his hand, and he was required to stand with bare feet in the bare grassless ground. The dedication of the young hunter was akin to those of the 'maor,' the judge, the chief, and the king, on installation. Many conditions were imposed on the young man, which he was required to observe throughout his life. He was not to take life wantonly. He was not to kill a bird sitting, nor a beast lying down, and he was not to kill the mother of a brood, nor the mother of a suckling. Nor was he to kill an unfledged bird nor a suckling beast, unless it might be the young of a bird, or of a beast, of prey. It was at all times permissible and laudable to destroy certain clearly defined birds and beasts of prey and evil reptiles, with their young.

From my loins begotten wert thou, my son,
May I guide thee the way that is right,
In the holy name of the apostles eleven
In the name of the Son of God torn of thee.

In the name of James, and Peter, and Paul,
John the baptist, and John the apostle above,
Luke the physician, and Stephen the martyr,
Muriel the fair, and Mary mother of the Lamb.

In the name of Patrick, holy of the deeds,
And Carmac of the rights and tombs,

Columba beloved, and Adamnan of laws,
Fite calm, and Bride of the milk and kine.

In the name of Michael chief of hosts,
In the name of Ariel youth of lovely hues,
In the name of Uriel of the golden locks,
And Gabriel seer of the Virgin of grace.

The time thou shalt have closed thine eye,
Thou shalt not bend thy knee nor move,
Thou shalt not wound the duck that is swimming,
Never shalt thou harry her of her young.

The white swan of the sweet gurgle,
The speckled dun of the brown tuft,
Thou shalt not cut a feather from their backs,
Till the doom-day, on the crest of the wave.

On the wing be they always
Ere thou place missile to thine ear,
And the fair Mary will give thee of her love,
And the lovely Bride will give thee of her kine.

Thou shalt not eat fallen fish nor fallen flesh,
Nor one bird that thy hand shall not bring down,
Be thou thankful for the one,
Though nine should be swimming.

The fairy swan of Bride of the flocks,
The fairy duck of Mary of peace.

81 *PRAYER FOR TRAVELLING*

This hymn was sung by a pilgrim in setting out on his pilgrimage. The family and friends joined the traveller in singing the hymn and starting the journey, from which too frequently, for various causes, he never returned.

Life be in my speech,
Sense in what I say,
The bloom of cherries on my lips,
Till I come back again.

The love Christ Jesus gave
Be filling every heart for me,
The love Christ Jesus gave
Filling me for every one.

Traversing corries, traversing forests,
Traversing valleys long and wild.
The fair white Mary still uphold me,
The Shepherd Jesu be my shield,
The fair white Mary still uphold me,
The Shepherd Jesu be my shield.

82 THE OCEAN BLESSING

Sea prayers and sea hymns were common amongst the seafarers of the Western Islands. Probably these originated with the early Celtic missionaries, who constantly traversed in their frail skin coracles the storm-swept, strongly tidal seas of those Hebrid Isles, oft and oft sealing their devotion with their lives.

Before embarking on a journey the voyagers stood round their boat and prayed to the God of the elements for a peaceful voyage over the stormy sea. The steersman led the appeal, while the swish of the waves below, the sough of the sea beyond, and the sound of the wind around blended with the voices of the suppliants and lent dignity and solemnity to the scene. . . .

83 SEA PRAYER

HELMSMAN   Blest be the boat.
CREW   God the Father bless her.
HELMSMAN   Blest be the boat.
CREW   God the Son bless her.

HELMSMAN	Blest be the boat.
CREW	God the Spirit bless her.
ALL	God the Father,
	God the Son,
	God the Spirit,
	Bless the boat.
HELMSMAN	What can befall you
	And God the Father with you?
CREW	No harm can befall us.
ALL	God the Father,
	God the Son,
	God the Spirit,
	With us eternally.
HELMSMAN	What can cause you anxiety
	And the God of the elements over you?
CREW	No anxiety can be ours.
HELMSMAN	What can cause you anxiety
	And the King of the elements over you?
CREW	No anxiety can be ours.
HELMSMAN	What can cause you anxiety
	And the Spirit of the elements over you?
CREW	No anxiety can be ours.
ALL	The God of the elements,
	The King of the elements,
	The Spirit of the elements,
	Close over us,
	Ever eternally.

MORNING PRAYERS

84 *THANKSGIVING*

Thanks to Thee, O God, that I have risen to-day,
    To the rising of this life itself;
May it be to Thine own glory, O God of every gift,
    And to the glory of my soul likewise.

O great God, aid Thou my soul
  With the aiding of Thine own mercy;
Even as I clothe my body with wool,
  Cover Thou my soul with the shadow of Thy wing.

Help me to avoid every sin,
  And the source of every sin to forsake;
And as the mist scatters on the crest of the hills,
  May each ill haze clear from my soul, O God.

85 GOD'S AID

God to enfold me,
  God to surround me,
God in my speaking,
  God in my thinking.

God in my sleeping,
  God in my waking,
God in my watching,
  God in my hoping.

God in my life,
  God in my lips,
God in my soul,
  God in my heart.

God in my sufficing,
  God in my slumber,
God in mine ever-living soul,
  God in mine eternity.

86 SUPPLICATION

The following poem was taken down from the recitation of Dugall MacAulay, cottar, Creagorry, Benbecula. MacAulay is an old man, full of old songs and hymns, runes and incantations, fairy stories and strange beliefs. These he heard from his aunt and mother, who were full of song and story, natural and supernatural, and of old lore of the most curious kind. . . .

> O Being of life!
> O Being of peace!
> O Being of time!
>> O Being of eternity!
>> O Being of eternity!
>
> Keep me in good means,
>> Keep me in good intent,
> Keep me in good estate,
>> Better than I know to ask,
>> Better than I know to ask.
>
> Shepherd me this day,
>> Relieve my distress,
> Enfold me this night,
>> Pour upon me Thy grace,
>> Pour upon me Thy grace!
>
> Guard for me my speech,
>> Strengthen for me my love,
> Illume for me the stream,
>> Succour Thou me in death,
>> Succour Thou me in death!

PRAYERS FOR PROTECTION

87 *THOU MY SOUL'S HEALER*

> Thou, my soul's Healer,
> Keep me at even,
> Keep me at morning,
> Keep me at noon,
> On rough course faring,
> Help and safeguard
> My means this night.

I am tired, astray, and stumbling,
Shield Thou me from snare and sin.

88 *ENCOMPASSING*

'Caim', encompassing, is a form of safeguarding common in the west. The encompassing of any of the Three Persons of the Trinity, or of the Blessed Virgin, or of any of the Apostles or of any of the saints may be invoked, according to the faith of the suppliant. In making the 'caim' the suppliant stretches out the right hand with the forefinger extended, and turns round sunwise as if on a pivot, describing a circle with the tip of the forefinger while invoking the desired protection. The circle encloses the suppliant and accompanies him as he walks onward, safeguarded from all evil without or within. Protestant or Catholic, educated or illiterate, may make the 'caim' in fear, danger or distress, as when some untoward noise is heard or some untoward object seen during the night.

The caim is called . . . the encompassing of God, of Christ, of the Spirit, of Mary, of the Holy Rood, of the Holy Rood and of the saints in heaven, of Michael, of the nine angels, of the saints and the nine angels, of Columba; and to these may be added the customary epithets, as . . . the encompassing of the God of the creatures, of Michael militant the victorious, of Columba the kindly. It is also called . . . the encompassing of the forefinger, and . . . the encompassing of righteousness.

The compassing of God and His right hand
Be upon my form and upon my frame;
The compassing of the High King and the grace of the Trinity
Be upon me abiding ever eternally,
    Be upon me abiding ever eternally.

May the compassing of the Three shield me in my means,
The compassing of the Three shield me this day,
The compassing of the Three shield me this night
From hate, from harm, from act, from ill,
    From hate, from harm, from act, from ill.

89 *ENCOMPASSING*

The compassing of God be on thee,
  The compassing of the God of life.

The compassing of Christ be on thee,
  The compassing of the Christ of love.

The compassing of the Spirit be on thee,
  The compassing of the Spirit of Grace.

The compassing of the Three be on thee,
  The compassing of the Three preserve thee,
  The compassing of the Three preserve thee.

JOURNEY PRAYERS, BLESSINGS AND INVOCATIONS

90 *THE GOSPEL OF CHRIST*

Reciter: Malcolm Sinclair, fisherman, Baile Phuill, Tiree.

This was the name of a charm worn upon the person to safeguard the wearer against drowning at sea, against disaster on land, against evil eye, evil wish, evil influences, against the wrongs and oppressions of man and the wiles and witcheries of woman, against being lifted by the hosts of the air, and against being waylaid by the fairies of the mound.

Such a charm might consist of a word, a phrase, a saying, or a verse from one of the Gospels, and from this came the name 'Gospel of Christ'. The words were written upon paper or parchment, and were often illuminated and ornamented in Celtic design, the script being thus rendered more precious by the beauty of its work and the beauty of its words.

The script was placed in a small bag of linen and sewn into the waistcoat of a man and the bodice of a woman, under the left arm. In the case of a child the bag was suspended from the neck by a linen cord. Linen was sacred because the body of Christ was buried in a linen shroud, and there are many phrases which indicate the special esteem in which lint was held. The blue flax was used medicinally, especially for stomach complaints, and also as a safeguard against invisible dangers. . . .

May God bless thy cross
    Before thou go over the sea;
Any illness that thou mayest have,
    It shall not take thee hence.

*

May God bless thy crucifying cross
    In the house-shelter of Christ,
Against drowning, against peril, against spells,
    Against sore wounding, against grisly fright.

As the King of kings was stretched up
    Without pity, without compassion, to the tree,
The leafy, brown, wreathed topmost Bough,
    As the body of the sinless Christ triumphed,

And as the woman of the seven blessings,
    Who is going in at their head,
May God bless all that are before thee
    And thee who art moving anear them.

*

Grace of form,
    Grace of voice be thine;
Grace of charity,
    Grace of wisdom be thine;
Grace of beauty,
    Grace of health be thine;
Grace of sea,
    Grace of land be thine;
Grace of music,
    Grace of guidance be thine;
Grace of battle-triumph,
    Grace of victory be thine;
Grace of life,
    Grace of praise be thine;

Grace of love,
　　Grace of dancing be thine;
Grace of lyre,
　　Grace of harp be thine;
Grace of sense,
　　Grace of reason be thine;
Grace of speech,
　　Grace of story be thine;
Grace of peace,
　　Grace of God be thine.

*

A voice soft and musical I pray for thee,
　　And a tongue loving and mild:
Two things good for daughter and for son,
　　For husband and for wife.

The joy of God be in thy face,
　　Joy to all who see thee;
The circling of God be keeping thee,
　　Angels of God shielding thee.

*

Nor sword shall wound thee,
Nor brand shall burn thee,
Nor arrow shall rend thee,
Nor seas shall drown thee.

*

Thou art whiter than the swan on miry lake,
Thou art whiter than the white gull of the current,
Thou art whiter than the snow of the high mountains,
Thou art whiter than the love of the angels of heaven.
Thou art the gracious red rowan
That subdues the ire and anger of all men,
　　As a sea-wave from flow to ebb,
　　As a sea-wave from ebb to flow.

*

The mantle of Christ be placed upon thee,
To shade thee from thy crown to thy sole;
The mantle of the God of life be keeping thee,
To be thy champion and thy leader.

*

Thou shalt not be left in the hand of the wicked,
Thou shalt not be bent in the court of the false;
Thou shalt rise victorious above them
As rise victorious the arches of the waves.

*

Thou art the pure love of the clouds,
Thou art the pure love of the skies,
Thou art the pure love of the stars,
Thou art the pure love of the moon,
Thou art the pure love of the sun,
Thou art the pure love of the heavens,
Thou art the pure love of the angels,
Thou art the pure love of Christ Himself,
Thou art the pure love of the God of all life.

91 *BLESSINGS*

Be each saint in heaven,
Each sainted woman in heaven,
Each angel in heaven
Stretching their arms for you,
Smoothing the way for you,
When you go thither
Over the river hard to see;
Oh when you go thither home
Over the river hard to see.

*

May the Father take you
In His fragrant clasp of love,
When you go across the flooding streams
And the black river of death.

*

The love of your Creator be with you.

*

Be the eye of God dwelling with you,
The foot of Christ in guidance with you,
The shower of the Spirit pouring on you,
     Richly and generously.

*

The love and affection of the heavens be to you,
The love and affection of the saints be to you,
The love and affection of the angels be to you,
The love and affection of the sun be to you,
The love and affection of the moon be to you,
     Each day and night of your lives,
     To keep you from haters, to keep you from harmers,
          to keep you from oppressors.

92 SUN

Old men in the Isles still uncover their heads when they first see the sun
on coming out in the morning. They hum a hymn not easily caught up
and not easily got from them. The following fragments were obtained
from a man of ninety-nine years in the south end of Uist, and from
another in Mingulay, one of the outer isles of Barra.

     The eye of the great God,
     The eye of the God of glory,
     The eye of the King of hosts,
     The eye of the King of the living,
          Pouring upon us
               At each time and season,
          Pouring upon us
               Gently and generously.

          Glory to thee,
               Thou glorious sun.

Glory to thee, thou sun,
Face of the God of life.

93 *CHARM FOR FEAR BY NIGHT*

This rune is said by travellers at night. Any person saying it from the heart will be sained and safeguarded from harm. He will not be molested by the 'fuath,' the 'gruagach,' the 'peallag,' the 'ban-sith,' the 'bean-nighidh,' nor by 'fridich nan creag,' not by any spirit in the air, in the earth, under the earth, in the sea, nor under the sea. The imprecation, 'Guma h-anmoch dhuit!', 'May you be late!' is still reckoned as specially evil. . . .

'Do you see anything, little son?' 'I see nothing, father.' 'Do you see anything now, little son?' 'I see nothing, father.' 'Do you see anything at all now, little son?' 'I see nothing at all, father.' 'By Mary, you see nothing! There is not so much sense in your head or in your snout or in your eye that you would see a bogle or anything else of the ill work of the night!'

This conversation took place between a father and the little son on his back as they were passing through a spot of evil reputation. When the father passed the dreaded hollow he put down his boy and ran as hard as he could. The boy overtook and passed him. When he reached home, the boy fell in the door exhausted. Immediatedly after the father came up and stumbled over the motionless boy lying in the doorway. Thinking that this was the bogle at last, the father yelled, rousing the boy without and the mother within. The frightened man gave his son a cuffing and a severe scolding for leaving him to the mercy of the bogles. . . . 'You little sack of hide, to go and leave your father to be eaten by the bogles of Lag Onair and the marsh-spirit of the night!'

God before me, God behind me,
God above me, God below me;
I on the path of God,
God upon my track.

*

Who is there on land?
Who is there on wave?
Who is there on billow?
Who is there by door-post?

Who is along with us?
　　God and Lord.

*

I am here abroad,
I am here in need,
I am here in pain,
I am here in straits
I am here alone,
　　O God, aid me.

94 *NIGHT PRAYER*

From Peigidh Nic Cormaig (Peggy MacCormack), *neé* MacDonald, Aird Bhuidhe, Loch Boisdale, Uist.

The reciter said that this and similar hymns used to be sung in her father's house at Airigh nam Ban in Uist. Crofters then held the land now occupied by sheep. The people were strong, healthy, and happy, and enjoyed life to the full in their simple homely ways. They had sheep and cattle, corn, potatoes, and poultry, milk, cheese, butter and fish, all in sufficiency. They were good to the poor, kind to the stranger, and helpful to one another, and there was nothing amiss. There were pipers and fiddlers in almost every house, and the people sang and danced in summer time on the green grass without, and in winter time on the clay floor within.

How we enjoyed ourselves in those far-away days — the old as much as the young. I often saw three and sometimes four generations dancing together on the green grass in the golden summer sunset. Men and women of fourscore or more — for they lived long in those days — dancing with boys and girls of five on the green grass. Those were the happy days and the happy nights, there was neither sin nor sorrow in the world for us. The thought of those young days makes my old heart both glad and sad, even at this distance of time. But the clearances came upon us, destroying all, turning our small crofts into big farms for the stranger, and turning our joy into misery, our gladness into bitterness, our blessing into blasphemy, and our Christianity into mockery. . . . O dear man, the tears come on my eyes when I think of all we suffered and of the sorrows, hardships, oppressions we came through.

In Thy name, O Jesu Who wast crucified,
    I lie down to rest;
Watch Thou me in sleep remote,
    Hold Thou me in Thy one hand;
        Watch Thou me in sleep remote,
        Hold Thou me in Thy one hand.

Bless me, O my Christ,
    Be Thou my shield protecting me,
Aid my steps in the pitful swamp,
    Lead Thou me to the life eternal;
        Aid my steps in the pitful swamp,
        Lead Thou me to the life eternal.

Keep Thou me in the presence of God,
    O good and gracious Son of the Virgin,
And fervently I pray Thy strong protection
    From my lying down at dusk to my rising at day;
        And fervently I pray Thy strong protection
        From my lying down at dusk to my rising at day.

95 *I LIE DOWN THIS NIGHT*

I lie down this night with God
    And God will lie down with me;
I lie down this night with Christ,
    And Christ will lie down with me;
I lie down this night with the Spirit,
    And the Spirit will lie down with me;
God and Christ and the Spirit
    Be lying down with me.

96 *REST BENEDICTION*

Reciter: Dugall MacAulay, cottar, Hacleit, Benbecula.

Bless to me, O God, the moon that is above me,
Bless to me, O God, the earth that is beneath me,

Bless to me, O God, my wife and my children,
And bless, O God, myself who have care of them;
     Bless to me my wife and my children,
     And bless, O God, myself who have care of them.

Bless, O God, the thing on which mine eye doth rest,
Bless, O God, the thing on which my hope doth rest,
Bless, O God, my reason and my purpose,
Bless, O bless Thou them, Thou God of life;
     Bless, O God, my reason and my purpose,
     Bless, O bless Thou them, Thou God of life.

Bless to me the bed-companion of my love,
Bless to me the handling of my hands,
Bless, O bless Thou to me, O God, the fencing of my defence,
And bless, O bless to me the angeling of my rest;
     Bless, O bless Thou to me, O God, the fencing of my defence,
     And bless, O bless to me the angeling of my rest.

97 *HAPPY DEATH*

. . . In the Roman Catholic communities of the west, 'bas sona,' 'happy death,' is a phrase frequently heard among the people. When these words are used they imply that the dying person has been confessed and anointed, and the death-hymn has been intoned over him. Under these conditions the consolation of the living in the loss of the loved one is touching. The old people speak of 'bas sona' with exultant satisfaction, and would wish above all things on earth that 'bas sona' may be their own portion when the time comes for them to go . . .

98 *JOYOUS DEATH*

     Death with oil,
     Death with joy,
     Death with light,
     Death with gladness,
          Death with penitence.

Death without pain,
Death without fear,
Death without death,
Death without horror,
    Death without grieving.

May the seven angels of the Holy Spirit
    And the two guardian angels
Shield me this night and every night
    Till light and dawn shall come;

        Shield me this night and every night
        Till light and dawn shall come.

The Religious Songs of Connacht:

A Collection of Poems, Stories, Prayers, Satires, Ranns, Charms etc.
being the Sixth and Seventh Chapters of
The Songs of Connacht

by Douglas Hyde

99 *MY SON REMEMBER*

After this necessary preface, we turn to the poems and religious songs themselves, which the people of Connacht had and have amongst them. That province gave to the nation the greatest and best religious poet that perhaps Erin has ever had, Donough O'Daly, who was, it was said, Abbot of Boyle, in the county of Roscommon, though this is not certain. The monastery of Boyle was a large and important institution; it scattered its branches east and west. The fine Abbey of Knockmoy, in the west of Galway, was only a branch from the Abbey of Boyle. But if the fame of the monastery was great, greater still was the fame of the Abbot who ruled over it in the beginning of the thirteenth century. The Abbot was called the Ovid of Erin, not for the freedom of his poetry, but for its sweetness. All Erin was proud of its splendid poet, Donagha More O'Daly. O'Reilly gives us the names of more than thirty of his extant poems, in which there are about 4,200 lines, and it is likely that there are more of his works which may yet be found. Most of these are religious poems, and they were held in high esteem throughout the Island. They were as well known in the province of Munster as they were in Connacht, and some of them are in the mouths of the people to this very day. I have heard from old people in the County Roscommon, his own county as it is believed, more than one of his pieces. He died in the year 1244. I shall here give only pieces of his that were very common in Ireland at the beginning of this century, and which are to be found in many of the manuscripts which, until lately, the people treasured in every part of Ireland, but which are now lost or banished.

Here, to begin, is a poem which he made, and which lived in the memory of the people for five hundred years; I got part of it from a "travelling-man" near Belmullet, in the west of the County Mayo, ten years ago. It is composed in the metre or measure called Great Rannuigheacht, [Rann-ee-ăcht]. There are seven syllables in the line, and each line must end with a monosyllable. There is no "Uaim" or alliteration in it, as there is in most of the poems which the true bards composed in this metre. Shaun O'Daly transcribed this poem from a collection which Father O'Keeffe (a learned man, and an accurate Irish scholar, born about the year 1655) made in Munster. Some of the lines of the original have eight syllables instead of seven, which is incorrect, but in my translation I have given each line this number.

MY SON REMEMBER

My son, remember what I *say*,
  That in the *day* of Judgment's shock,
When men go stumbling down the *Mount*,
  The sheep may *count* thee of their flock.

And narrow though thou find the path
  To heaven's high rath, and hard to gain,
I warn thee shun yon broad white road
  That leads to the abode of pain.

For us is many a snare designed,
  To fill our mind with doubts and fears;
Far from the land where lurks no sin
  We dwell within our vale of tears.

Not on the world thy love bestow,
  Passing as flowers that blow and die;
Follow not thou the specious track
  That turns thy back to God most high.

But oh! let faith, let Hope, let love
  Soar far above the cold world's way;
Patience, humility, and awe —
  Make them thy law from day to day.

And love thy neighbour as thyself,
    (Not for his pelf thy love should be),
But a greater love than every love
    Give God above who loveth thee.

He shall not see the abode of pain
    Whose mercies rain on poor men still;
Arms, fastings, prayers, must aid the soul;
    Thy blood control, control thy will.

The seven shafts wherewith the Unjust
    Shoots hard, to thrust us from our home,
Can'st thou avoid their fiery path,
    Dread not the wrath that is to come.

Shun sloth, shun greed, shun sensual fires,
    (Eager desires of men enslaved),
Anger and pride and hatred shun,
    Till heaven be won, till man be saved.

To Him, our King, to Mary's son,
    Who did not shun the evil death,
Since He our goal is, He alone,
    Commit thy soul, thy life, thy breath.

Since Hell each man pursues each day,
    Cleric and lay, till life be done,
Be not deceived, as others may,
    Remember what I say, my son.

100 *THE WORMS, THE CHILDREN, AND THE DEVIL*

Although O'Reilly gives us this poem amongst those of Donogha More's he says that he has cause for believing that it was not he who composed it. The following is my version of it. Shaun O'Daly printed a different copy of it in his book of the songs of "Teig O Sullivan the Gaelic," and he says it was Donogha O'Daly wrote it. It is in the Great Rannuigheacht metre.

THE WORMS, THE CHILDREN, AND THE DEVIL

There be three — my heart it saith —
    Wish the death of me infirm,
Would that they were hanged on tree,
    All three, Children, Devil, Worm.

The worms — it is a sad thought —
    When I am brought under clay,
My body they make their goal,
    For wealth or soul nought care they.

My children care for my wealth
    More than my health, when all's done,
They'd give, to get its control,
    My body and soul in one.

The loathly devil, I wis,
    Whose business is to sow tares,
Not for body, not for gold,
    Only for my soul he cares,

Now O Christ, for us who died,
    Crucified upon the tree,
These three wait for me to die,
    Swing them high in death all three.

101 BRIDGET'S COUNSEL

. . . most of the religious poems which I have got from the people in Connacht are giving us advice to do good works, and saying that there is no road but this by which a man may go to the heaven of God. Here for example is a poem which I wrote down from the mouth of a man in the county Galway. Martin Rua O Gillarná (Forde! in English) was his name. He was from Lisanishka near Monivea. He had no English.

BRIDGET'S COUNSEL

The teaching of Breed for his good to the sinner,
To take his father's advice and blessing,
To plead for ever with Mary Mother,
A guiding-star to our foolish women.

The Son of the Woman who earned no scandal,
The Son who never forgot the Father,
It was He himself who made our purchase,
And through His side that the lance's thrust went.

The poem goes on to say of those who have no pleasure in alms or in
mercy: —

The darkest night in this world at present
Dark without mist or stars or moonlight,
Is brighter than their day when brightest.

Could you come with me but once, and see it,
You would sooner be hacked in little pieces,
Be boiled, be burned, and be roasted,

Be put in an oven till you had perished,
Be ground in a quern with hundreds grinding,
— Sooner than live in a sin that is mortal.

Go to Mass when you rise at morning,
As you should do, regard the altar.
See, Christ Jesus is thereby standing,
In the priest's hand is His sacred body.

Go home again when that is finished,
Give wanderers lodging until the morning,
Food and drink to him who is empty.

Is your friend ill, or on sick-bed lying,
Bring him whatever will give him comfort,
— Never earn the curse of widow.

147

When to your bed you get at night-time
Go on your knees your prayers repeating,
Do the same when you rise next morning.

What the poem chiefly teaches is to do good deeds: —

Do good deeds without lie or falsehood,
Do without lie good deeds on earth here,
That is the one straight way to follow,
That is the road, and go not off it.

102 *MARY'S WELL*

If we look around us, over the lands of Christendom today, we shall
scarcely see another place in which the love and respect of their people
for the priesthood is greater than in Erin. I am not now speaking of any
cause of quarrel that may have lately come between them, but if we
examine the history of the country during the last couple of hundred years
we find that the priest clung to his people, and the people to their priest.

The long years, full of ruin and poverty, which the Irish suffered after
the downfall of their natural protectors, the native nobles, without
anyone to stand up for them but their own priests, bound them to the
heart of the nation, strongly, firmly, inseparably. The people saw
during two hundred years their priests in poverty and misery, standing
in the gap of danger, seeking to fulfil their sacred office, coming in and
going out amongst them, anointing those who were on the point of
death, tying young couples, assuaging the grief of the poor, and
administering the sacraments of the church, although they themselves
often met suffering and persecution and death in doing so. If what I
have just said is true, namely, that there is scarce another country in
Europe in which the respect for and power of the Roman Catholic
priests is as great as it is in Erin, and if we seek what is the cause, we shall
easily understand that it is because Erin has not yet forgotten all the
misfortunes and persecutions which she and her priests suffered together during the penal laws. She has not yet quite forgotten it; and if
the priesthood of Erin has so good a position, in comparison with the
Roman Catholic priests of other countries, it is not on account of Celtic
blood being in the people, nor on account of anything else of the sort,
but on account of the comfort, the satisfaction, the aid, and the

continuous- help which the poor people of Erin received from their priests in the last two centuries, when there was not other person of education taking their part, but they only.

The wiles which the priests of Erin had to practice in order to save their lives are not yet forgotten. But these old stories are passing into dis-remembrance since the priests and the people begin to cast away from them the Irish language, in which they were told. There were people at one time in Ireland who had no other business than to find out priests and gain from the law a reward on account of their dirty work, as we see from this rann which Father O'Leary heard from some one.

> There is no use in my speaking [encomiums on you]
> Seeing your kinsip with Donogha-of-the-priest,
> And with Owen-of-the-cards, his father,
> With the people of the cutting off of the heads,
> To put them into leather bags,
> To bring them down with them to the city,
> and to bring home the gold [they got for them]
> For sustenance of wives and children.

Here is a story, for example, which I got from Próinsias O'Conor, in Athlone, who heard it from an old woman who was herself from Ballintubber, in the County Mayo. So long as Irish was spoken, and these stories told in it it was small wonder that the people should have a regard for their priests.

MARY'S WELL

Long ago there was a blessed well in Ballintubber (i.e., the town of the well), in the county Mayo. There was once a monastery in the place where the well is now, and it was on the spot where stood the altar of the monastery that the well broke out. The monastery was on the side of a hill, but Cromwell and his band of destroyers came to this country, they overthrew the monastery, and never left stone on top of stone in the altar that they did not throw down.

A year from the day that they threw down the altar — that was Lady Day in spring — the well broke out on the site of the altar, and it is a wonderful thing to say, but there was not one drop of water in the stream that was at the foot of the hill from the day that the well broke out.

There was a poor friar going down the road the same day, and he

149

went out of his way to say a prayer upon the site of the blessed altar, and there was great wonder on him when he saw a fine well in its place. He fell on his knees and began to say his paternoster, when he heard a voice saying: 'Put off your brogues, you are upon blessed ground, you are on the brink of Mary's well, and there is the curing of thousands of blind in it; there shall be a person cured by the water of that well for every person who heard mass in front of the altar that was in the place where the well is now, if they be dipped three times in it, in the name of the Father, the Son, and the Holy Spirit.'

When the friar had his prayers said, he looked up and saw a large white dove upon a fir tree near him. It was the dove who was speaking. The friar was dressed in false clothes, because there was a price on his head, as great as on the head of a wild-dog.

At any rate, he proclaimed the story to the people of the little village, and it was not long till it went out through the country. It was a poor place, and the people in it had nothing [to live in] but huts, and these filled with smoke. On that account there were a great many weak-eyed people amongst them. With the dawn, on the next day, there were above forty people at Mary's Well, and there was never a man nor woman of them but came back with good sight.

The fame of Mary's Well went through the country, and it was not long till there were pilgrims from every county coming to it, and nobody went back without being cured; and at the end of a little time even people from other countries used to be coming to it.

There was an unbeliever living near Mary's Well. It was a gentleman he was, and he did not believe in the cure. He said there was nothing in it but pishtrogues (charms), and to make a mock of the people he brought a blind ass, that he had, to the well, and he dipped its head under the water. The ass got its sight, but the scoffer was brought home as blind as the sole of your shoe.

At the end of a year it so happened that there was a priest working as a gardener with the gentleman who was blind. The priest was dressed like a workman, and nobody at all knew that it was the priest who was in it. One day the gentleman was sickly, and he asked his servant to take him out into the garden. When he came to the place where the priest was working he sat down. 'Isn't it a great pity,' says he, 'that I cannot see my fine garden?'

The gardener took compassion on him, and said, 'I know where there is a man who would cure you, but there is a price on his head on account of his religion.'

'I give my word that I'll do no spying on him, and I'll pay him well for his trouble,' said the gentleman.

'But perhaps you would not like to go through the mode of curing that he has,' says the gardener.

'I don't care what mode he has, if he gives me my sight,' said the gentleman.

Now, the gentleman had an evil character, because he betrayed a number of priests before that. Bingham was the name that was on him. However, the priest took courage, and said, 'Let your coach be ready on to-morrow morning, and I will drive you to the place of the cure; neither coachman nor anyone else may be present but myself, and do not tell to anyone at all where you are going, or give anyone a knowledge of what is your business.'

On the morning of the next day Bingham's coach was ready, and he himself got into it, with the gardener driving him. 'Do you remain at home this time,' he says to the coachman, 'and the gardener will drive me.' The coachman was a villain, and there was plenty of jealousy on him. He conceived the idea of watching the coach to see what way they were to go. His blessed vestments were on the priest, inside of his outer clothes. When they came to Mary's Well the priest said to him, 'I am going to get back your sight for you in the place where you lost it.' Then he dipped him three times in the well, in the name of the Father, the Son, and the Holy Spirit and his sight came to him as well as ever it was.

'I'll give you a hundred pounds,' said Bingham, 'as soon as I go home.'

The coachman was watching, and as soon as he saw the priest in his blessed vestments, he went to the people of the law, and betrayed the priest. He was taken and hanged, without judge, without judgment. The man who was after getting back his sight could have saved the priest, but he did not speak a word on his behalf.

About a month after this, another priest came to Bingham, and he dressed like a gardener, and he asked work of Bingham, and got it from him; but he was not long in his service until an evil thing happened to Bingham. He went out one day walking through his fields, and there met him a good-looking girl, the daughter of a poor man, and he assaulted her, and left her half dead. The girl had three brothers, and they took an oath that they would kill him as soon as they could get hold of him. They had not long to wait. They caught him in the same place where he had assaulted the girl, and hanged him on a tree, and left him there hanging.

On the morning of the next day millions of flies were gathered like a great hill round about the tree, and nobody could go near it on account of the foul smell that was round the place, and anyone who would go near it the midges would blind him.

Bingham's wife and son offered a hundred pounds to anyone who would bring out the body. A good many people made an effort to do that, but they were not able. They got dust to shake on the flies, and boughs of trees to beat them with, but they were not able to scatter them, nor to go as far as the tree. The foul smell was getting worse, and the neighbours were afraid that the flies and noisome corpse would bring a plague upon them.

The second priest was at this time a gardener with Bingham, but the people of the house did not know that it was a priest who was in it, for if the people of the law or the spies knew, they would take him and hang him. The Catholics went to Bingham's wife and told her that they knew a man who would banish the flies. 'Bring him to me,' said she, 'and if he is able to banish the flies, that is not the reward he'll get, but seven times as much.'

'But,' said they, 'if the people of the law knew, they would take him and hang him, as they hung the man who got back the sight of his eyes for him before.' 'But,' said she, 'could not he banish the flies without the knowledge of the people of the law?'

'We don't know,' said they, 'until we take counsel with him.'

That night they took counsel with the priest and told him what Bingham's wife said.

'I have only an earthly life to lose,' said the priest, 'and I shall give it up for the sake of the poor people, for there will be a plague in the country unless I banish the flies. On to-morrow morning I shall make an attempt to banish them in the name of God, and I have hope and confidence in God that he will save me from mine enemies. Go to the lady now, and tell her that I shall be near the tree at sunrise to-morrow morning, and tell her to have men ready to put the corpse in the grave.'

They went to the lady and told her all the priest said.

'If it succeeds with him,' said she, 'I shall have the reward ready for him, and I shall order seven men to be present.'

The priest spent that night in prayer, and half an hour before sunrise he went to the place where his blessed vestments were hidden; he put these on, and with a cross in one hand, with the holy-water in the other, he went to the place where were the flies. He then began reading out of his book and scattering holy-water on the flies, in the name of the Father, the Son, and the Holy Ghost. The hill of flies rose, and flew up into the air, and made the heaven as dark as night. The people did not know where they went, but at the end of half an hour there was not one of them to be seen.

There was great joy on the people, but it was not long until they saw the spy coming, and they called to the priest to run away as quick as it was in him to run. The priest gave to the butts (took to his heels), and the spy followed him, and with a knife in each hand with him. When he was not able to come up with the priest he flung the knife after him. As the knife was flying out past the priest's shoulder he put up his left hand and caught it, and without ever looking behind him he flung it back. It struck the man and went through his heart, so that he fell dead and the priest went free.

The people got the body of Bingham and buried it in the grave, but when they went to bury the body of the spy they found thousands of rats round it, and there was not a morsel of flesh on his bones that they had not eaten. They would not stir from the body, and the people were not able to rout them away, so that they had to leave the bones over-ground.

The priest hid away his blessed vestments and was working in the garden when Bingham's wife sent for him, and told him to take the reward that was for banishing the flies, and to give it to the man who banished them, if he knew him.

'I do know him, and he told me to bring him the reward to-night, because he has the intention of leaving the country before the law-people hang him.'

'Here it is for you,' she said, and she handed him a purse of gold.

On the morning of the next day the priest went to the brink of the sea, and found a ship that was going to France. He went on board, and as soon as he had left the harbour he put his priest's-clothes on him, and gave thanks to God for bringing him safe. We do not know what happened to him from that out.

After that, blind and sore-eyed people used to be coming to Mary's Well, and not a person of them ever returned without being cured. But there never yet was anything good in this country that was not spoilt by somebody, and the well was spoilt in this way.

There was a girl in Ballintubber and she was about to be married, when there came a half-blind old woman to her asking alms in the honour of God and Mary.

'I've nothing to give an old blind-thing of a hag, it's bothered with them I am,' said the girl.

'That the marriage ring may never go on you until you're as blind as myself,' says the old woman.

Next day, in the morning, the young girl's eyes were sore, and the morning after that she was nearly blind, and the neighbours said to her that she ought to go to Mary's Well.

In the morning, early, she rose up and went to the well, but who should she see at it but the old woman who asked the alms of her, sitting on the brink, combing her head over the blessed well.

'Destruction on you, you nasty hag, is it dirtying Mary's well you are?' said the girl, 'Get out of that or I'll break your neck.'

'You have no honour nor regard for God or Mary, you refused to give alms in honour of them, and for that reason you shall not dip yourself in the well.'

The girl caught hold of the hag, trying to pull her from the well, and with the dragging that was between them, the two of them fell into the well and were drowned.

From that day to this there has been no cure in the well.

103 *GREAT MARY*

Mary Mother bears a great part in the religious poetry of the Gaels. It was she who put the curing of the blind in the well, it was she who showed herself to the poor friar under the form of a dove, and it is she who gives a cure to the poor of the world through her intercession with her Son. It was no wonder, then, that the heart of the Gaels, the heart of a nation that especially respected and honoured its women, should give itself up particularly to Mary.

    'Good is the woman, Great Mary,'
says Owen O'Duffy,
    'A Woman who give sight to the blind.'

GREAT MARY

Good is the woman, Great Mary,
The mother of the High-king of the eternal hosts,
They are her graces which are ever full,
A woman who put a hedge around each country.

A woman to whom right inclines,
A woman greatest in strength and power,
A woman softest (i.e., most generous) in red gold,
A woman by whom is quenched the anger of the king.

A woman who gives sight to the blind,
A woman who is most powerful beyond in heaven,
A woman who has taken away my enemies from me,
A woman who is a defence to me in every battle.

[. . .]

Mary is not like women,
[Great Mary of good deeds],
Balsam is not like to myrrh,
To salt ale, wine is not like.

Gall is not like honey,
And brass is not like gold,
The lily is not like the thorn,
And to smooth plain, bog is not like.

104 *CHARM AGAINST EVIL EYE*

The belief is very common in Ireland and in Scotland that there are people in it who can cast an evil eye on anything that they please. If they cast an evil eye on your churn there will be no butter in the churning, if they cast it on your cow perhaps she will fall and be hurt, if they cast it on yourself perhaps it is a heavy disease or sickness that will come upon you. Here is a charm against the evil eye that Mr. Lyons wrote from the mouth of a man from Donegal, and Father O'Growney found the same charm in Aran.

CHARM AGAINST EVIL EYE

God's Son hath given a charm of charms,
    (First on thy knees thy *pater* say),
Shed was His blood by cruel arms,
    Faultless and fair his righteous sway.

When Mary saw him, as she stood,
  High on the Cross all torn and rent,
Rained from her eyes three showers of blood
  And at its foot she made lament.

An Evil Eye hath me undone
  Paling my face in dule and dree,
I cry to Mary and her Son
  Take the ill eye away from me.

105 *I PRAY GOD'S RIGHT-HAND ANGEL*

Father Eugene O'Growney, of a day, met a little child in Aran, and they were talking to one another, until at last they talked about fairies, and the child spoke to him exactly thus, 'It is said Father,' says he, 'anything that is seen on your left-hand side, — that it is a bad thing, but anything that will rise up on your right-hand side — it is no danger to you. But, whatever side they rise on, here is a charm to be said against them going the way, of you.'

I PRAY GOD'S RIGHT-HAND ANGEL

I pray the Right-hand Angel of God
That he may put me on the best-way for me,
I pray for God's sake
The Left-hand Spirits
    All of them, so let me be.

106 *CHARM AGAINST FAIRIES*

Here is another little charm I heard from Father O'Growney against the fäerie of the fairies.

We accept their protection
And we refuse their removal,
Their back to us,
Their face from us,
Through the death and passion
Of our Saviour Jesus Christ.

107 *TO SAINT PATRICK*

Here is another melodious little song in honour of St. Patrick, which I got from the same Patrick O'Donnell. I do not remember that I ever heard any other verses in honour of St. Patrick amongst the people except this one — a thing which surprises me.

> O Patrick in the Paradise
> Of God on high,
> Who lookest on the poor man
> With a gracious eye,
> See me come before thee
> Who am weak and bare,
> O help me into Paradise
> To find thee there.

108 *A BLIND MAN'S CURSE*

A curse is a sort of prayer also; it is an evil prayer. I have not up to this given any example of these; but it is worth while to put down a few of them, and — 'may God increase the good, and diminish the evil' — it is out of no bad intention I am doing it, but only to preserve a specimen of every kind. This book would not be complete without one or two of them being in it. Curses are not numerous. When a person frames a prayer for himself, praying to God and Mary, his prayer is suitable for thousands of other people; but it is not so with the curse. It only appertains to the person who shaped it, and the person against whom it is loosed. The prayer suits the public; the curse concerns only the special person. I never heard any rhymed curse in the mouths of the people — a curse going the country, so to speak, and it ready to be launched at the enemy. I do not think there is such a thing. But here is an example or two of how people composed their own curses for themselves, when they sought to overthrow their opponents.

There was a poor blind man seeking alms in the County Galway, and he came to the door of a big house, and asked for a drink. The woman of the house was an English (or English-speaking?) woman, and since she did not understand him, she asked the servant what was the blind man asking for. The servant told her that he was asking for a drink. *'Water is good enough for the blind beggar,*' said she. The blind man understood the thing she said, and answered: —

A BLIND MAN'S CURSE

Your milk may no butter crown,
On your ducks may there come no down,
May your child never walk the ground,
    Be your cows where the flayer flays.
May more hot be in the flames that shall roll
One day through your wicked soul
Than the mountains of Connemara
    And they be in one blaze.

109 *THE BED CONFESSION*

Here is a version of the 'Bed Confession' that I heard in the county Mayo. There is a good deal of this that I had not got before, and it is worth while putting it down entirely.

May we lie down with God, and may God lie with us.
A Person from God with us. The two hands of God with us.
The Three Marys with us.
God and Columcille with us.
Is it not strong the fortress in which we are!
Between Mary and her Son,
Brigit and her mantle,
Michael and his shield,
God and His right hand,
Going between us and every evil.
May we not lie down with evil,
May evil not lie down with us.
The protection of the Three Trees,
The tree of the Cross,
The tree of the blood,
The tree on which Christ was hanged
And from which He rose again alive.
O King of the *cathair* in heaven,
Keep the spirit of my soul
From the real-temptations of the adversary.

110 *A HEALTH*

Here is a curious health from the County Mayo which I got from my friend Philip Waldron of Drombaun, about three miles from Ballyhaunis: —

> A health let us drink. Our glass we clink it,
>   May the King of the Graces to us be near.
> We will drink this glass as Patrick would drink it,
>   With a grace made salt by a mingled tear,
> Without sadness or sorrow or passion or pain,
>   — None knowing to-morrow that we were here.

Here is another little prayer in which Patrick is mentioned: —

THE LUCK OF GOD AND PROSPERITY OF PATRICK

> The luck of God and the prosperity of Patrick on all I shall see, and on all I shall touch, from the time I rise at morning until I sleep at night.

111 *HOW THE FIRST CAT WAS CREATED*

Here is a curious story that I got from my friend Dr. Connor Maguire, of Claremorris. I believe he got it from Ned Gibbons, the same old man from whom I got that fine poem, 'The Joyce's Repentance.' This story explains how the first cat and the first mouse were created. I heard many of such stories from the Red Indians in Canada, giving us to understand how this thing or the other thing was first made, but none of them had anything to say to Christianity! It is impossible to tell what is the age of this story, but it is certain that stories of this kind were common in early pagan times, even as they are common now amongst the Red men, and other wild tribes; and it may be that the story is older than the Christian religion itself, and that a saint was first put in the place of an enchanter when people began to become Christians. I think it is certain that this story originally concerned only the flour — the food of man — and the mice — the enemy of the flour — and the cat — the enemy of the mice; and the mention of the sow and her litter is a late and stupid introduction. This is only a supposition, and I shall set down the story here without saying any more and without altering anything in it.

HOW THE FIRST CAT WAS CREATED

One day Mary and her Son were travelling the road, and they heavy and tired, and it chanced that they went past the door of a house in which there was a lock (a small quantity) of wheat being winnowed. The Blessed Virgin went in, and she asked an alms of wheat, and the woman of the house refused her.

'Go in again to her,' said the Son, 'and ask her for it in the name of God.'

She went, and the woman refused her again.

'Go into her again,' said He, 'and ask her to give you leave to put your hand into the pail of water, and to thrust it down into the heap of wheat, and to take away with you all that shall cling to your hand.'

She went, and the woman gave her leave to do that. When she came out to our Saviour He said to her, 'Do not let one grain of that go astray, for it is worth much and much.'

When they had gone a bit from the house they looked back, and saw a flock of demons coming towards the house, and the Virgin Mary was frightened lest they might do harm to the woman. 'Let there be no anxiety on you,' said Jesus to her; 'since it has chanced that she has given you all that of alms, they shall get no victory over her.'

They travelled on, then, until they reached as far as a place where a man named Martin had a mill. 'Go in,' said our Saviour to his mother, 'since it has chanced that the mill is working, and ask them to grind that little grain-*een* for you.'

She went. 'O musha, it's not worth while for me,' said the boy who was attending the querns, 'to put that little lock*een* a-grinding for you.' Martin heard them talking and said to the lout, 'Oh, then, do it for the creature, perhaps she wants it badly,' said he. He did it, and he gave her all the flour that came from it.

They travelled on then, and they were not gone any distance until the mill was full of flour as white as snow. When Martin perceived this great miracle he understood well that it was the Son of God and His Mother, who chanced that way. He ran out and followed them, at his best, and he made across fields until he came up with them, and there was that much haste on him in going through a scunce (a thick-set double ditch) of hawthorns that a spike of the hawthorn met his breast and wounded him greatly. There was that much zeal in him that he did not feel the pain, but clapt his hand over it, and never stopped until he came up with them. When our Saviour beheld the wound upon poor Martin He laid his hand upon it, and it was closed, and healed upon the spot. He said to Martin then that he was a fitting man in the presence of God, 'and go home now,' said He, 'and place a fistful of flour under a dish, and do not stir it until morning.'

When Martin went home and did that, and he put the dish, mouth under, and the fistful of flour beneath it.

The servant girl was watching him, and thought that maybe it would be a good thing if she were to set a dish for herself in the same way, and signs on her, she set it.

On the morning of the next day Martin lifted his dish, and what should run out from under it but a fine sow and a big litter of bonhams with her. The girl lifted her own dish, and there ran out a big mouse and a clutch of young mouselets with her. They ran here and there, and Martin at once thought that they were not good, and he plucked a big mitten off his hand and flung it at the young mice, but as soon as it touched the ground it changed into a cat, and the cat began to kill the young mice. That was the beginning of cats. Martin was a saint from that time forward, but it is not known which of the saints he was of all who were called Martin.

Modern Poetry

INTRODUCTION

Artistic inspiration is often born from tension, the attempt of individuals to make sense of, articulate and come to terms with disparate elements of their experience. For 'Celtic' poets writing today the relationship between the past and present is a rich, if somewhat vexed, vein to tap. Questions of identity, language, nationhood and of one's relationship to the land and community pose particular conundrums in an increasingly cosmopolitan world. A nostalgic sentimentality, evident in some nineteenth-century verse, is usually eschewed, and we see an often ambivalent attitude towards the past and the ties of family and tribal loyalty. There are also, however, aspects of contemporary poetry from the Celtic countries which echo themes evident in the medieval period. An attachment to the land, not in general, but to a particular country, hill, valley, rock, island or town, is striking; not a romanticized, idealized landscape, but actual places which the poets know and value for their own sake. There is no doubting, for instance, that Ian Crichton Smith, born on the Hebridean island of Lewis, is writing of a specific place and a familiar experience in his poem 'By Ferry to the Island':[1]

> We crossed by ferry to the bare island
> where sheep and cows stared coldly through the wind—
> the sea behind us with its silver water,
> the silent ferryman standing in the stern
> clutching his coat about him like old iron.

There is ambivalence about these island roots, however, evident in Crichton Smith's poem 'Going Home':[2]

> Tomorrow I shall go home to my island . . .
> I will lift a fistful of its earth in my hands
> or I will sit on a hillock of the mind
> watching 'the shepherd at his sheep'.

There will arise (I presume) a thrush.
A dawn or two will break . . .

Ian Crichton Smith, like so many of his fellow Gaelic language poets
in Scotland, is in exile from his home, and to some extent from the
language community that raised him. The forces described by Alexander Carmichael which drove the Gaels from their native villages,
valleys and islands are still operating. The old saying that Glasgow is the
capital of the Highlands and Islands of Scotland (and Liverpool and
London respectively of north and south Wales) are not without meaning today. The same is not true, however, of the Breton poet Anjela
Duval. She lived almost all her life in the family farmhouse, working the
same few acres of land. Some of her more nationalistic verse shares with
Anglo-Welsh poet, R. S. Thomas, a deep anxiety at the encroachment
of foreigners into that beloved land, as in 'Work of the Foreigner':[3]

Strip. Despoil our Country
Sweep away the sacred oaks of the Druids
The birches of the Celts and the yew-trees
— And the chestnuts of our youth —
In which our birds sang.

More characteristic of Duval's poems, however, is a celebration of her
relationship with nature, a ubiquitous subject for what are in the main
rural poets, as in her poem 'Lindens'. Having described the thirteen
giant trees, already full grown in her youth, Duval reveals her inner
attitude to the land she inherited from her parents:

These lindens are not my possession
Yet I possess the right
To cut them down
They are sucking the sap of my land
With their roots so long. But I won't.
I would miss them
For they are part of that living tableau
That forms the framework of my life.

Nature is characteristically allowed to be just that, the natural world.
Where it is invested with meaning beyond its surface appearance, this is
usually the sense of wonder and astonishment invoked in the human

observer by the simple fact that it exists, and exists not just in the eyes and minds of human beings but for its own sake. The Scottish poet Edwin Muir in 'Horse' describes his fascination with the shire horses he used to watch ploughing the rocky fields of his childhood:[4]

> Those lumbering horses in the steady plough
> On the bare field — I wonder why, just now,
> They seemed terrible, so wild and strange,
> Like magic power on the stony grange.

In her poem 'A Marvellous Hour', Duval describes the tranquillity of evening after a day's work, 'The hour of prayer, hour of study./Hour of dreaming, of fantasy,/Hour divine, full of ecstasy'. All that the poet misses to perfect the moment is the singing of a cricket in the hearth. Gillian Clarke's description of the birth of a calf on a hot summer's day, in her poem 'Birth', has the quiet and empathetic observation of something that is in itself a miracle: the gift of new life.[5]

> . . . Hot and slippery, the scalding
> Baby came, and the cow stood up, her cool
> Flanks like white flowers in the dark.
> We waited while the calf struggled
> To stand, moved as though this
> Were the first time. I could feel the soft sucking
> Of the new-born, the tugging pleasure
> Of bruised reordering, the signal
> Of milk's incoming tide, and satisfaction
> Fall like a clean sheet around us.

One of the tensions evident in medieval verse is the relationship between Christianity and the pre-Christian past or 'pagan' elements in the present. This relationship between the past and present, and the Christian/pagan mixture of religious traditions and sensibilities, is sometimes evoked through a sense of place. The topographical features of the landscape and human endeavours which leave their mark for later generations can be 'read' by those sensitive to them. Gillian Clarke and Seamus Heaney were both struck by the little squat carved stone figure of a fertility goddess (Sheelagh na Gig) on the twelfth-century church at Kilpeck in Herefordshire. In Gillian Clarke's memorable words (in her poem 'Sheila na Gig at Kilpeck'):[6]

Pain's a cup of honey in the pelvis.
She burns in the long, hot afternoon, stone
among the monstrous nursery faces
circling Kilpeck church.

Ruth Bidgood in her poem 'Hoofprints' describes the way in which 'carved hoofprints on a rock' acquire mythological significance:[7]

The legend was always here,
at first invisible, poised above the hill,
stiller than any kestrel . . .

And so it remains until people recognize in the marks the leap of a magic horse, 'the print of miracle'. Similarly in 'Green Man at the Bwlch', Bidgood describes the serendipity which brought the Green Man to her conscious attention until at last she discovers him in a remote half-crumbled house:[8]

In a central room, on the beam
over the great hearth, royally
he spreads his mouth-borne branches,
meets my unsurprised eyes . . .

The terror is in his utter
neutrality. Yet somewhere
in his kingdom of possibilities
is a tree whose leaves give shelter,
whose boughs know songs, whose sap
flows gold through our veins.

A sense of community, not only with the living, but also with the dead, is another recurrent motif in both medieval and contemporary Celtic verse. Death, in fact, seems to hold a particular fascination for the Celts. George Mackay Brown's extraordinarily evocative poem 'The Jars' recalls a man's life in a dream-like state which hovers between the living and the dead. His family, his loves and labours are distilled into jars found in a deserted house. For Euros Bowen the Christian theology of death and resurrection, sometimes perceived in terms of failure and triumph, are subsumed into an older, more ecologically balanced, affirmation that life and death belong together, and that all life depends

upon the earth which sustains us. 'The earth keeps the tap root of death awake . . . /Without a root in the earth death's finality is our death . . . /
There is no resurrection where there is no earth.' Brendan Kennelly is another poet keenly aware of the continuity between the living and the dead. At the end of his poem 'House' he writes:[9]

> Listen! You can hear the dance
> Starting on the kitchen floor.
> They are learning the steps
> Becoming the music
> Reaching the skill, the fever,
> Doing what I've always wanted.
> Dancing through me, dancing their beginning,
> They are learning to be haunted.

For Ruth Bidgood keeping faith with the dead involves a recitation of the names of farms and houses, now mainly deserted. In 'All Souls' this act of remembrance takes on the strains of a litany:[10]

> From the hill Clyn ahead
> Glangwesyn's lively shout of light
> celebrates old Nant Henfron, will not let
> Cenfaes and Blaennant be voiceless.
> I am a latecomer, but offer
> speech to the nameless, those
> who are hardly a memory, those
> whose words were always faint
> against the deafening darkness
> of remotest hills.

Anjela Duval describes her heart as a cemetery containing the countless graves of friends and relatives but, like Ruth Bidgood, transforms the finality of the past through remembrance. The poem 'My Heart' ends with this transformation:

> My heart is a Cemetery
> But no!
> My heart is a Sanctuary
> Wherein live My Dear Departed!

Contemporary Celtic poets also deal with the living community, often with those marginalized and ignored by our modern society which values outward achievements and material success above all. In 'Down Syndrome, in memory of Joseph Leary', Bernard O'Donaghue writes 'Take consolation that it won't be you/That has to declare strategy/Or give the order to burn sprawling/Ranks of soldiers.' Joseph Leary, instead, had 'a weakness for the truth', and an ability to bring out the best in those who knew him.[11] In 'St Magnus Day in the Island' and 'Feast of Candles' George Mackay Brown celebrates the community, ordinary working Orkney people with their rough hands and faces, long-suffering and enduring, who gather together for ritual, pilgrimage and worship.[12]

> (And the monk gathered the folds of his cloak
> together at the altar and bent
> and prayed between two tall
> set apart candles: in Latin
> whispers and a boy replied,
> hesitant with the Latin syllables,
> in country whispers)
> And a flame set, and a flame set, and a flame
> set . . .

An emphasis on community is linked, very often, to an awareness of presence (or absence). Space is not empty but resonant. Material objects which might at first sight appear fixed yield to subtler dimensions, change form and take on meanings beyond their surface solidity. Even when dealing with everyday occurrences and the most mundane realities, such as eating Christmas dinner with relatives, the poet remains sensitive to the possibility of less visible company. Angels, fairies, spirits of nature and of the dead are never far away, and whether one 'believes in' them or not, they continue to inhabit the poetic imagination. This ever present other world is strongly felt in much of Nuala Ní Dhomhnaill's powerful poetry. In 'Abduction', for instance, the housewife changes place with a fairy woman:[13]

> The fairy woman walked
> into my poem.
> She closed no door
> She asked no by-your-leave.

Knowing my place
I did not tell her to go.

Nuala Ní Dhomhnaill's 'Parthenogenesis' recalls Irish legends of the coupling of a woman with a mysterious sea creature while she is out swimming, subsequently giving birth to a child of the 'Sea People':

She and her husband so satisfied,
so full of love for this new son
forgot the shadow in the sea
and did not see what only the midwife saw —
stalks of sea-tangle in the boy's hair
small shellfish and sea-ribbons
and his two big eyes
as blue and limpid as lagoons.

For R. S. Thomas in 'The Presence' the invisible world is not named or peopled with miraculous creatures but is no less strongly felt:[14]

I feel the power
that, invisible, catches me
by the sleeve . . .
I know its ways with me;
how it enters my life,
is present rather
before I perceive it, sunlight quivering
on a bare wall.

The human community, past and present, with this Celtic admixture of ordinary human foibles and ancient mystery, is captured by John Montague in his poem 'Like Dolmens Round My Childhood, the Old People'.[15] The figures of the poet's youth are named, Jamie MacCrystal who 'sang to himself a broken song, without tune, without words'. Maggie Owens, surrounded by animals, the Nialls who 'lived along a mountain lane' and who were all blind. Mary Moore, who is remembered for her 'bag apron and boots'. This, however, seems to be a community which is failing to renew itself: 'Sometimes they were found by neighbours,/Silent keepers of a smokeless hearth,/Suddenly cast in the mould of death.' The ambivalence shown towards a rural island home in Ian Crichton Smith's poetry is echoed in Montague's observation of the dying, inward-looking community of his youth. His poem ends with a kind of exorcism which brings personal realease, but which at the same time links his present with his past, and with the past of all the people of Ireland:

> Ancient Ireland, indeed! I was reared by her bedside,
> The rune and the chant, evil eye and averted head,
> Fomorian fierceness of family and local feud.
> Gaunt figures of fear and of friendliness,
> For years they trespassed on my dreams,
> Until once, in a standing circle of stones,
> I felt their shadows pass
> Into that dark permanence of ancient forms.

Miracle, in many different guises, expresses the poet's vision of the world. It could be described in terms of the tension between the ordinary and extraordinary, everyday reality and that particular vision which makes the mundane special and the inanimate alive. Nuala Ní Dhomhnaill's poem 'Marvellous Grass' is reminiscent of the stories of miracle-working priests with supernatural powers collected by Douglas Hyde in his *Religious Songs of Connacht*.

> When you were a holy priest
> in the middle of Mass in your purple robes
> your linen mantle, your stole, your chasuble.
> You saw my face in the crowd
> approaching you for communion
> and you dropped the blessed host . . .
>
> And in the place where fell
> the sacred host you will see
> among the useless plants
> a patch of marvellous grass.

Religion as a theme in the poems selected here is interpreted broadly — a yearning of the human spirit, a proclivity to wonder and the company of a world infused with glory. As an explicit subject religion, or Christianity, is oriented less towards creeds and the dogmas of faith (which are more often expressed in hymns) than to experience and theophany — the birds, animals, flowers, and even the humble lichen offer their sacrament of praise to the Creator. There are some poems of more traditional piety, such as Anjela Duval's 'Saint Mary' which echoes both the Magnificat and the Prayer of Saint Francis ('Saint Mary, Mother of God,/Preserve for me a child's heart,/Pure and transparent as a spring,/A heart simple and straight,/That will never taste unhappiness . . .'), or John F. Deane's poem 'Contact'.[16]

> *When I call to you, God,*
> *it is only that I want to grasp*
> *what you can offer; when you call to me,*
> *God, I know you want*
> *all that I have to offer, so,*
> *I yield to the distractions.*
>   *. . . Now,*
> *if I can only find the silence,*
> *a sudden glance towards you*
> *can be my prayer.*

Pilgrimage, whether ancient or contemporary, and tales of Celtic saints, are frequent subjects for many Celtic poets. Norman MacCaig turns to Assisi, while George Mackay Brown focuses on the popular Highland saint, St Magnus. John Irvine imagines Colm-Cille's farewell to his native Ireland before setting sail for Iona in his poem 'Saint Colm Cille and the Cairn of Farewell' which, with its rather sentimental nostalgia and simple rhyme, recalls the exile of so many of Ireland's sons and daughters today:[17]

> The oaks are green in Derry now,
> The waves break on the Irish shore,
> My grief that I must say farewell —
> Farewell for ever more . . .
>
> But row me to Iona's Isle
> Though I am weary of the sea,
> Beyond the far enpurpled hills
> That will not let me be.

Both Sheenagh Pugh, writing about St Cuthbert, and Nuala Ní Dhomhnaill, referring to St Anthony, speculate on the hermit's relationship with women and on the narrow asceticism which feeds on misogyny. In Nuala Ní Dhomhnaill's poem 'Monk' the torments suffered by the ascetic are not related to individual, particular women, as in Sheenagh Pugh's 'St Cuthbert and the Women', but to the feminine ('Eve' and 'the serpent') and to the very forces of life itself:[18]

> But it's not to torment you
> every day I rise —
> but to drown you
> in love's delights.
> I'm a dead hero leaping
> from the edge of the bridge of fear —
> That's the only reason I haunt you:
> my monk, my apostle, my priest.

Ambivalence in religion is a frequent contemporary preoccupation. The exuberant confidence of the medieval 'Loves of Taliesin', and of many oral invocations recorded by Alexander Carmichael, do not have the self-conscious quality which characterizes R. S. Thomas' verse. In 'Covenant' the poet states 'I feel sometimes we are his penance for having made us', and ends with the words:[19]

> Often
> I think that there is no end
> to this torment and that the electricity
> that convulses us is the fire
> in which a god
> burns and is not consumed.

Another clergyman, Euros Bowen, seems at times unsure of his loyalties to a patriarchal God who requires us to be his human servants. The goddess, in the guise of Gaia or the earth, is bemoaned now that she is all but destroyed. In 'Changing Government' Bowen writes:[20]

> We no longer put our trust
> in the masculine deity
> of the mountain and the sea
> nor in the feminine deity
> of rivers and trees . . .

The queen of heaven has been divorced,
she is throneless in our world
now that the ridges of her ramparts
are in laboratories . . .

With the change to
our government
the writing of the four winds is on the wall,
for the rocks cannot become bread
and the waters
cannot turn the air into wine.

The poetic tradition and the magic power of language sometimes evoked in medieval verse continues to preoccupy contemporary Celtic poets. The way in which the poet becomes a mere channel for a higher power is beautifully captured by W. R. Rogers in the poem 'Words'. The words arrive like 'winds', pouring like 'Atlantic gales over these ears', waiting in the darkness of the unconscious to come forth and 'speak for me — their most astonished host'.[21] In Gillian Clarke's poem 'Miracle on St David's Day' it is poetry which reawakens speech in a man long silent, joining human verse to the paeans of the flowers and the thrush:[22]

He is suddenly standing, silently,
huge and mild, but I feel afraid. Like slow
movement of spring water or the first bird
of the year in the breaking darkness,
the labourer's voice recites 'The Daffodils'.

The nurses are frozen, alert; the patients
seem to listen. He is hoarse but word-perfect.
Outside the daffodils are still as wax,
a thousand, ten thousand, their syllables
unspoken, their creams and yellows still.

Forty years ago, in a Valleys school,
the class recited poetry by rote.
Since the dumbness of misery fell
he has remembered there was a music
of speech and that once he had something to say.

When he's done, before the applause, we observe
the flowers' silence. A thrush sings
and the daffodils are flame.

The harsher realities of life are not forgotten by other Celtic poets, even in their religious verse. On seeing a military jet over the west Wales countryside Gillian Clarke, in her poem 'In January', muses that:[23]

The cities can forget on days like this
all the world's wars. It's we
out on the open hill who see
the day crack under the shadow of the cross.

And in 'Fires on Llyn', Clarke describes sitting with a friend at Uwchmynydd on the edge of the Llyn Peninsula in Gwynedd, looking out towards Bardsey Island (Ynys Enlli), the resting place of 'twenty thousand saints', and to Ireland beyond:[24]

Facing west, we've talked for hours
of our history,
thinking of Ireland and the hurt
cities,
gunshot on lonely farms,

praised unsectarian saints,
Enlli open
to the broken rosary
of their coracles,
praying in Latin and Welsh.

The Ulster-born poet Louis MacNeice ends his famous poem 'Prayer Before Birth', which is a great cry for justice and truly human values, with the words:[25]

I am not yet born; O fill me
With strength against those who would freeze my
    humanity, would dragoon me into a lethal automaton,
        would make me a cog in a machine, a thing with
            one face, a thing, and against all those

who would dissipate my entirety, would
blow me like thistledown hither and
thither or hither and thither
like water held in the
hands would spill me.

Let them not make me a stone and let them not spill me.
Otherwise kill me.

Notes

1 *Thistles and Roses*, Eyre & Spottiswode 1961.
2 *Nua-Bhardachd Ghaidhlig/Modern Scottish Gaelic Poems*, Canongate 1980. The translation is by the author.
3 All the quotations of the work of Anjela Duval are from *A Modern Breton Political Poet: Anjela Duval*, edited and introduced by L. A. Timm, Edwin Mellen 1990. The translations from Breton are by Lenora Timm.
4 From *First Poems*, 1925, reprinted in *Edwin Muir's Collected Poems, 1921-1958*, Faber & Faber.
5 *Selected Poems*, Carcanet, London 1985.
6 ibid.
7 *The Print of Miracle*, Gomer 1978.
8 Ruth Bidgood, *Selected Poems*, Seren/Poetry Wales Press 1992.
9 *Breathing Spaces*, Bloodaxe 1992.
10 *The Print of Miracle*.
11 *The Weakness*, Chatto & Windus 1991.
12 *The Wreck of the Archangel*, John Murray 1989.
13 *Selected Poems: Rogha Dánta*, Raven Arts Press 1991. English translations in this bilingual edition are by Michael Hartnett. All the poems by Nuala Ní Dhomhnaill are taken from this edition.
14 *Between Here and Now*, Macmillan 1981.
15 *The Rough Field*, Dolmen Press 1972.
16 *The Deer's Cry*, edited by Patrick Murray, Four Courts Press 1986.
17 ibid.
18 *Selected Poems*, Seren (Poetry Wales Press) 1992.
19 *Between Here and Now*.
20 *Priest-Poet/Bardd-Offeiriad*, Church in Wales Publications 1993; translation by Cynthia Davies.
21 *Collected Poems*, Oxford University Press 1971.
22 *Selected Poems*.
23 *Letting in the Rumour*, Carcanet 1989.
24 *Selected Poems*.
25 *The Deer's Cry*.

SAUNDERS LEWIS (1893–1985)

Saunders Lewis, poet, playwright, nationalist and scholar, was a somewhat enigmatic character who often occupied the lonely and anomalous position of the insider/outsider. Born and brought up in Cheshire, where his father was minister to a Welsh-speaking chapel, he was sent to a minor English public school. He studied English and French at Liverpool University, and developed a life-long love of France. Saunders Lewis' decision to join the Roman Catholic Church (in 1932) was linked to his sense of continuity with a pan-European medieval Catholic culture. From 1923–36 Saunders Lewis lectured in Welsh at the University of Wales, Swansea, and began writing plays in Welsh, despite the fact that the Welsh theatrical tradition was virtually non-existent. In 1925 Saunders Lewis was one of the founder members of the Welsh Nationalist Party, Plaid Cymru, *and its President from 1926–1939. A radio talk by Lewis on the fate of the Welsh language in 1962 was instrumental in the founding of the Welsh Language Society,* Cymdeithas yr Iaith Gymraeg. *Saunders Lewis was briefly imprisoned and was dismissed from his post at Swansea for his part in a symbolic demonstration against English rule in Wales in 1936. It was not until 1952 that the Welsh Department in Cardiff offered him work.*

112 *ASCENSION THURSDAY*

What is happening this May morning on the hillside?
See there, the gold of the broom and laburnum
And the bright surplice on the thorn's shoulder
And the intent emerald of the grass and the still calves;

See the candelabra of the chestnut tree alight
The bushes kneel and the mute beech, like a nun,
The cuckoo's two notes above the bright hush of the stream,
And the form of the mist that curls from the censor of the meadows.

Come out, you men, from the council houses
Before the rabbits run, come with the weasel to see
The elevation of the unblemished host from the earth,
The Father kiss the Son in the white dew.

EUROS BOWEN (1904–1988)

Euros Bowen was brought up in the Rhondda Valley in south Wales. He was son of a Congregationalist minister, and intended to follow his father's profession, but after studying in various places in Wales and in Oxford he joined the Anglican Church, and served as a priest of the Church in Wales. Euros Bowen was a prolific poet in Welsh. He wrote both in free verse and in cynghanedd *(strict metre), and twice won the crown at the National Eisteddfod. In 1974 Bowen translated some of his own poems into English (some of which are included here). Although widely educated in classical and French literature (which he also translated), and strongly attracted to Eastern Christianity, Euros Bowen's poetry owes more to the medieval Welsh tradition. The sacramentality of nature and the place of humanity within the world are recurrent themes in his verses.*

113 THE ROWAN TREE

You can see it above the river's hollow bank, on the edge,
      of gorse and wind,
A crack in bareness of rock is its earth.

The twisted form of its grey trunk stands,
      gaunt and bare,
Shaped like a wooden cross.

Its branches are arms outstretched, darkened
      by a wound in the chest,
Rough and harsh as the ribs of Christ.

And blood trickles on this tree, on the edge
      of gorse and wind,
Blood which breaks from the swell of God's pity.

114 *THIS IS PRAISE*

In my day I have often heard morning and evening
the thrush's call
on the tree's high branch,
the brook trebling in the solitude
of moor-bank and marsh,
an infant's ready laughter
at his foot's first venture on the ground,
and the children's noisy fun
on the village meadow:
And when the swallow,
its diligent nesting done,
has left for the south,
I have seen summer decay
as an acorn rolls golden
into the shadow of the country's oak,
like the smile of the departed
before burial in the earth. —
Life does not die. This is praise.

115 *REREDOS*

The reredos was not
an ecclesiastical adornment
of symbols,
but plain glass,
with the danger
of distracting the celebrant
from
the properties of the communion table.

for
in the translucence
the green earth
budded in the morning view,
the river was in bloom,
the air a joyous flight,

and the sunshine
set the clouds ablaze.

and I noticed
the priest's eyes
as it were unconsciously
placing his hand
on these gifts,
as though these
were
the bread and the wine.

116 *CROWS*

Crows flying to their retreat in the woods' choir,
turning away beyond the road's rushing,
old ever-with-us-things
like green, yellowish grey sins,
the generations of the leaves and the oak trees' decay,
ministers under the raucous belfry of the parish,
in their black despite the broken altars of the druids,
as it now between the surpliced walls of heaven
chanting the psalms of the day's meditations —
having long been shepherding the salt of the earth
in the light of the world on slope and on field,
listening to the treasure's seed
and pecking to the very heart
of the hidden wisdom between the rocks and the stones, —
and returning from the ravines' fragrances
to chancel and altar at nightfall
past the ebb and the flow, the ashes and the dust
with the mustard seeds of the pearl in their beak, —
the stewards of the blessed mysteries
under the hill's bells in the branched glory of the tree.

117 *CHANGING GOVERNMENT*

We no longer put our trust
in the masculine deity
of the mountain and the sea
nor in the feminine deity
of rivers and trees.

The government of the skies
we have sent to hell,
and so the throne of the sun is empty;
there is a death mask on its face
in a museum.

The queen of heaven has been divorced,
she is throneless in our world
now that the ridges of her ramparts
are in laboratories.

By now
the traces of the carriages
of their splendour
across the day
and across the night skies
have become the sphere of archaeology.

In the midst of our century
a desert of dust exploded
between us and the sceptre of light,
and we the subjects of
goodness
were found
in a heap of rubble.

Under our government
the privy council of the stars were all excommunicated.

The brightness on the sea
is the spittle of oils,

slag-heaps are filth's poison,
and the gold of the heavens is lead
that fouls lungs wings and leaves.

They are at it desecrating the sea's care,
polluting the river's cleanliness;
the wells were deprived of their healing power
and the generosity of the trees was demythologized.

Chapter and verse
the manna and the miracle
in the west and the east,
in the north and the south,
in unscriptural language
in the marrow
and the blood's mouth.

With the change to
our government
the writing of the four winds is on the wall,
for the rocks cannot become bread
and the waters
cannot turn the air into wine.

118 *A REFRIGERATOR*

A cupboard
the buttress of technology
in the kitchen,
a very material and useful
refuge:
keeping together
the mild of meadows,
the pasture's honey,
the produce of fields and forests,
the goodness
of the cream and the mill,
the generosity
of the wine vat.

All that was conceived
by the air
and the earth
in the graves of the soil
and that was nurtured
by water
and fire
in the cradle of the earth
is born anew:

The trout's resurrection
beside the descents of the valley,
the salmon's leap
by the falls of the weir,

the firmament's power
gladdens

the slopes of the lemon,
breezes
sweetening the juice of oranges.

This is the culture of the sun's galleries
and the utterance of the rain's pastures:

The store cupboard
of the anamnesis
of the images of earth.

119 *TAP ROOT*

The earth keeps the tap root of death
    awake:

The flesh covering bones will rot,
    or, if it does not, will remain
    as stone relics
    eventually
    for antiquarians,
    fragments of a city under a heap.

The flesh of leaves will descend into oblivion,
  blood filled limbs becoming clay,
  veins of branches clotting coldly.

Without a root in the earth
  death's finality is our death,
  like snowflakes on a river's current,
  like birds' designs in the sky:

There is no resurrection where there is no earth.

120 *MOUNTAINS*

We had better leave these mountains
where they are
to their fate and the wind.

If we were to shepherd them
with our years,
that would make no scrap of difference
to their shape and colour
as mountains.

Although, probably, the outcrop
of their shape and colour
would leave its mark
on the flesh and bone
of the days that belong to us.

For their outline is to us an assurance
of the stability of rock
and a warrant of the blade of tenderness
in that heritage
that is faith under the wind's roar,
the faith
that does not want to move mountains.

GEORGE MACKAY BROWN (b.1921)

George Mackay Brown comes from an old Orkney family and, apart from a period studying at Edinburgh University, has lived most of his life in Orkney. He joined the Roman Catholic Church in 1961. Some of Brown's most memorable works feature Saint Magnus, patron saint of Orkney, and detail the relationship between religion and the harsh life of the island people, as in the following passage from 'Our Lady of the Waves':

> Blessed Lady, since midnight
> We have done three things
> We have bent hooks,
> We have patched a sail.
> We have sharpened knives,
> Yet the little silver brothers are afraid.
> Bid them come to our net,
> Show them our fire, our fine round plates.
> *Per Dominum Christum nostrum*
> Look mildly on our hungers.

As well as poetry, Brown has written short stories, plays, novels, essays, books for children and a non-fictional work on Orkney. Together with religion, it is the physical environment of his island home and the interweaving of Scots and Norse myths and cultures which provide the main inspiration for his poetry.

121 *THE JARS*

A house on the mist-shrouded moor! —
the ghost of a house

Over the lintel this carving
HOUSE OF WOMEN

Not a woman stirred, outside
or in

He knocked. No-one answered.
He pushed open the door

It was dark and cold inside
the house

He opened a cupboard. In the
cupboard was a small clay
jar with markings on it

He tasted the stuff in the jar:
finest of honey! His flesh
glowed with lost suns and
blossoms. He sipped again

Now the window was black
as tar

He stooped. He stroked with
blind hands the shape of a bed.
He covered himself with coarse
weave

He slept at once

                *   *   *

The man woke. The window
was gray. He took down the jar
to taste the honey

The single jar stood on the shelf —
the shape of it had changed, and it
was of coarser clay

He opened it. It was crammed
with salt.

(the man heard, somewhere in
the house, a small cry)

He went through the rooms
of the house in search of a
child. The house was empty still

He returned to the room with
the cupboard and jar. He said,
*Young one, whoever you are, you
won't starve because of me —
There will be fish for the salting*

He came to a room where
the hearth was cold and the
lamp empty

On a stone of the wall was
carved the shape of a fish

He looked at the rune so long
that it seemed to pass into him
and become part of him

In another room, hidden, a
girl was singing

The man said, *Lost and
darkling creature, I will bring
you oil and driftwood
always*

The song guttered out. It
stopped. It faltered into
low cries of pain

*   *   *

The man wandered again
through the rooms of the house

He saw his reflection in a
pane. Furrows in the face,
a mesh of gray through his
black beard

A poor house, he said.
There should be a bowl
on the sill, daffodils
or roses or heather, to say
what time of year it is — yes —
to spill some beauty into a
bleak place. This jar is all,
it seems

He took the jar from the shelf.
An earth smell came out of it —
it was half full of flailed corn.
His hands that held the jar were
twisted with a summer of pain

Through the corridors of the
house a contented cry came. It
must (he thought) be a woman over
new loaves and ale, well pleased,
arms and face fire-flushed

Lost one in this house, he
said, *there will always be*
cornstorks — I will see to it

He scratched an ear-of-corn
on a stone beside the stone
with the carved fish

*   *   *

He lay down on the bed.
He was as weary as if he
had toiled, sunrise to
sunset, in a harvest field

He lay under a green and
a gold wave

His dream was about the
one jar that flowed always
from shape to shape, and
was ripeness, keeping, care,
sorrow, delight

The man woke. He knew now
that he was old

A thin-spun silver flowed over
the blanket. His hands were like
shreds of net, or winter roots

Seven women of different
ages stood about his bed. They
all, from first to last, had the
same fleeting look: the lost
girl at the horse fair

One by one, beginning with
the youngest, they bent over
and kissed him

The mid-most woman smelt
of roses and sunlight. Her
mouth had the wild honey
taste

The oldest one dropped
tears on his face

Then the seven women
covered their faccs and
went out of the room

* * *

He slept on into the starred
ebb of winter

*   *   *

He opened his eyes

A young man was
standing in the open door. He
carried a jar on his
shoulder

The young man greeted
him — then he turned
and went out into the
sun

The man said, *That is
my son. He is carrying
away the dust of my death*

RUTH BIDGOOD (b.1922)

Ruth Bidgood was born at Seven Sisters near Neath in south Wales, and was educated in Wales and Oxford. After many years and a varied career in England she went to live in the hamlet of Abergwesyn near Llanwrtyd Wells on the eastern edge of the Cambrian Mountains. She writes with great sensitivity of people, both living and dead, known personally and through records in local archives. Her poems refer chiefly to the places and people in her immediate locality, including her own family, and to the minutiae of nature which frequently reveal the awe-inspiring wonders of the creation. Ruth Bidgood's poems are sacramental rather than sentimental. Her touch is light and often humorous and gives the impression of a writer who has made peace with herself and with life.

122 *THE SPOUT*

Rain and rain had followed snow.
Under watery sun, sluggish water
spread, slid on the hill-slope:
churned narrow, brown in ditches:
sucked our steps between tussocks.
The river went in new white violence
over the rocks and down.

The children were tired of wet plodding.
Fields were rutted, grey-brown,
a mess of plashiness; one only,
steeply tilted, showed green.
Thankful for easy walking,
we idled across it.

Just before the gate, we saw grasses
gleam and part. A newborn spout

sprang up, sparkled, flowed.
It spoke to the children. They laughed, screamed,
bathed muddy hands, patted the spout,
attacked it, tried to force it back down,
jumped on it, over it, into it.

A skyful of water, a landful of water,
a dayful of water; and the little spout
could do this! The dismal downwardness
of mud, cheating slitheriness
of surface puddles, demented downrush
of rivers, were gathered, embraced, redeemed
by the small eager spout,
the thrusting, humorous creature of water,
that irrepressibly proclaimed
upwardness, happy intransigence,
in the depth of things.

123 SOURCES
a. County History
Llangynog

Small, bleak and barren,
with a ruinous church,
wrote the historian, apologising
for noting a place devoid
of history or good soil,
whose few frugal farmers
would gaze down mortified
from their snowy hills
at the soft flocking-in of green
to the spring valley.

Cold and late in greyness,
over a field of wet red earth
I draggle to barbed wire
and a ditch. Beyond the trees
Cynog's roofless church

suffers a long shedding of stone.
I free an earthbound cross,
prop it against rubble.
Wind seeps through shelter-trees.
Consecrated silence welcomes in
a flock of prayers crying,
praises clapping their wings.

124 *RESURRECTION ANGELS*

(Kilvert was told that the people used to come to the Wild Duck Pool
on Easter morning 'to see the sun dance and play in the water and the
angels who were at the Resurrection playing backwards and forwards
before the sun'.)

These were not troubling the waters
to bring healing. They were serving
no purpose. After the watch at the tomb,
the giving of good news, they were at play.
To and fro went the wings, to and fro
over the water, playing before the sun.

Stolid-seeming villagers stared
enchanted, watching sun dance and play,
light-slivers splinter water's dark.
In dazzle they half-saw
great shining shapes swoop frolicking
to and fro, to and fro.
                    This much was shared,
expected; day and place had their
appropriateness, their certainties.
The people had no words to tell
the astonishment, the individual bounty —
for each his own dance in the veins,
brush of wings on the soul.

125 *ALL SOULS'*

Shutting my gate, I walk away
from the small glow of my banked fire
into a black All Souls'. Presently
the sky slides back across the void
like a grey film. Then the hedges
are present, and the trees, which my mind
already knows, are no longer
strangers to my eyes.
The road curves. Further along,
a conversation of lights begins
from a few houses, invisible except as light,
calling to farms that higher in darkness
answer still, though each now speaks
for others that lie dumb.
Light at Tymawr above me, muted by trees,
is all the voice Brongwesyn has,
that once called clearly enough
into the upper valley's night.
From the hill Clyn ahead
Glangwesyn's lively shout of light
celebrates old Nant Henfron, will not let
Cenfaes and Blaennant be voiceless.
I am a latecomer, but offer
speech to the nameless, those
who are hardly a memory, those
whose words were always faint
against the deafening darkness
of remotest hills.
For them tonight when I go home
I will draw back my curtains, for them
my house shall sing with light.

126 *STANDING STONE*

The stone stands among new firs,
still overtopping them. Soon

they will hide it. Their lower branches
will find its cold bulk
blocking their growth. After years,
lopped trunks will lie piled,
awaiting haulage. The stone will stand
in a cleared valley, and offer again
the ancient orientation.

The stone stores, transmits.
Against its almost-smoothness
I press my palms. I cannot ask,
having no word of power,
no question formed. Have I
anything to give? My hands offer
a dumb love, a hope towards
the day of the freed valley.
Flesh fits itself to the slow curve
of dominating stone, as prayer
takes the shape of a god's will.

A mindless ritual is not empty.
When the dark minds fails, faith lives
in the supplication of hands
on prayer-wheel, rosary, stone.
It is evening. I walk down-valley
on an old track. Behind me
the ephemeral trees darken.
Among them, the stone waits.

127 *DRINKING STONE*

You offer me your stories
laughing, to show I may laugh, to say
you are sure I must mock
at such old childishness.
Tonight by your fire I listen
to tales of the drinking stone
that each midsummer cockcrow
goes thirsty down to the stream.

I am not to think you credit
that shuddering heave of stone
from the suck of earth, that gliding
over still-dark fields, that long drinking.
You tell it laughing, wary of my response,
but I shall not think you credulous.
It is I who thirstily drink
wonders, I who from dawn mist mould
a grey shape, sated, going home.

128 *HOOFPRINTS*

The legend was always here,
at first invisible, poised above the hill,
stiller than any kestrel. Idle hands
carved hoofprints on a rock
by the hill path. The legend, venturing nearer,
breathed warm as blessing. At last
men recognised it. A magic horse
had leapt from hill to hill, they said,
the day the valley began. Could they not see
his prints, that had waited in the rock
till guided hands revealed them?
From the unseeable, legends leap.
In the rock of our days
is hidden the print of miracle.

129 *LAST WORDS*

They came for his last counsel,
saying 'Tell us now, tell us,
sum your life for us before you go.
we need the right question,
the sufficient answer.'

He turned his head stiffly on the pillow,
and muttered of a curving wall
and moss on stone, of wind in the hedge

by the top gate, the stir and trample
of uneasy mares. He whispered
of a russet hill across the river,
and on the bank one golden tree.
'It is too late,' they said,
'he is babbling.' They touched his hand,
and went away.

He felt the resistance of stone,
the fragile antennae of moss
and its plushy deeps. He heard
a breeze in the hazel, and soft snorting
of gentled mares. At the river,
whirl upon whirl rose over him
the golden leaves, a visual song,
balance of phrase and phrase,
question and answer.

130 *LICHEN, CLADONIA FIMBRIATA*

This little scaly thing,
fibrous lichen, taker of peat-acid
the rotten juice of dead trees,
grows lowly, slowly, on bog-earth
or the scant soil of crevices,
and holds up to the air its fruit
in tiny fantastic goblets.

Might not this pallid creeping thing,
that needs for food only the sour,
sparse and corrupt, be late to go? —
too small and too tenacious
to be torn off by the dusty wind
and offering in final celebration
its little tainted chalices?

131 *GREEN MAN AT THE BWLCH*

For a week or more
some baffling serendipity
has brought him to me
in books, journals, photographs —
a play-mouthed face,
flesh shared with leaves.

Now on a remote pass above trees
of two Radnor valleys
I come to this ancient place —
cruck house half-crumbled, lovingly encased
by scaffolding and plastic sheets, cocoon
in which goes on the work of rebirth.
He is here too.

In a central room, on the beam
over the great hearth, royally
he spreads his mouth-borne branches,
meets my unsurprised eyes.
Here is an abyss, like Nietzsche's,
into which if I look long
I find it looking into me.

The terror is in his utter
neutrality. Yet somewhere
in his kingdom of possibilities
is a tree whose leaves give shelter,
whose boughs know songs, whose sap
flows gold through our veins.

132 *LOTUS*

Bryn, the round hill,
dips to a valley that accepts
others: a place of joining.
No wind carries up

conversation of rivers.
Old sheepwalks, hardly grazed,
stretch to the verge of forest.
On this grey day
no smoke rises
from the one gaunt house.

Surely the silent utterance
of this place is 'Emptiness',
its time 'Never'?
Yet it is said
that not leaves, not petals,
but the space at the centre
of the heart's lotus
contains everything.
                                    Here
rivers out of sight
have their rhythms,
like blood through the heart.
Stillness throbs with the flow
of unperceived lives.

This is a place of joining,
whose silent utterance is 'Abundance',
whose time is 'Ever'.

133 *ROADS*

No need to wonder what heron-haunted lake
lay in the other valley,
or regret the songs in the forest
I chose not to traverse.
No need to ask where other roads might have led,
since they led elsewhere;
for nowhere but this here and now
is my true destination.
The river is gentle in the soft evening,
and all the steps of my life have brought me home.

W. R. ROGERS (1909–1969)

W. R. Rogers was born in Belfast and graduated from Queen's University, before entering the Presbyterian ministry. In 1946 Rogers moved to London to work for the BBC, and spent the rest of his life in England and California. As well as poetry and his work as a journalist, Rogers wrote scripts for radio.

134 *WORDS*

Always the arriving winds of words
Pour like Atlantic gales over these ears,
These reefs, these foils and fenders, these shrinking
And sea-scalded edges of the brain-land.
Rebutted and rebounding, on they post
Past my remembrance, falling all unplanned.
But some day out of darkness they'll come forth,
Arrowed and narrowed into my tongue's tip,

And speak for me — their most astonished host.

GLADYS MARY COLES

Gladys Mary Coles was educated at Liverpool University, where she now teaches a creative writing course, travelling from her home on Deeside in north Wales. Coles has written biography as well as poetry. Places, particularly with historical or mythological significance, feature widely in her work, and the landscape of north Wales is a frequent source of inspiration.

135 *WATER POWER*

Sacred Well

Cures and curses
and counter-curses —
this well's water
accepted all wishes:

Send a baby to Gwen's womb.
Please untie my stammer.
Cure Alun's black hairy tongue.
Make Edward Hughes love me
and let a sore spread
in the middle of Nell Parry's face.

Dropped into depths —
medieval believings.
    Stick a pin
    in a cork:
    throw it in.
    Rub a rag on rheumatics:
    dip it in.
    Rub rheumatics on the rag:
    hang it high.
Trees near the well
festooned with shreds
of hopes.

Earlier still,
a Roman at Sulis Minerva
cast his lead tablet in:
May he who carried off Vilbia
from me, become as liquid as water.
Only the God could read the curse —
its backward flow.

I come today with my own petitions,
seeking the well on Llanelian hill:
Let all terrorists' bombs
explode in their faces.
Give rapists the rot.
Protect us from Poll's evil eye.
Please clear my writer's block.

The hills are green heaven,
the sky a blue halo,
I look for the well at Llanelian —
no fold in a field yields a sign,
only weeds crowd the meadow —
Llanelian's landlord has filled it in.

I leave with my ill-wishings,
well-wishings.

BRENDAN KENNELLY (b.1936)

Brendan Kennelly was born in Ballylongford, County Kerry (Ireland), and educated in Kerry and at Trinity College Dublin, where he worked for many years, being appointed Professor of Modern Literature in 1973. Kennelly is a prolific writer in many genres, including plays and poetry. His engagement with poetry involves a wrestling with the Irish psyche. People make outcasts, he suggests, of what is most exciting and most revealing, and 'in Ireland, this outcasting, this silent, fierce partitioning of energies is so commonplace as to be unobserved'. The Irish, he suggests, fall back too readily on labels and clichés, which give a spurious sense of security, and it is the task of the poet to fight 'their muggy, cloying, complacent, sticky, distorting, stultifying, murderous and utterly reassuring embrace'.* In this Kennelly succeeds magnificently. His poetry is refreshing, surprising, moving and often haunting — always honest and never self-indulgent; carefully crafted with an easy narrative style.

136 *SCULPTED FROM DARKNESS*

It is one o'clock on a Christmas morning.
The people are passing over the bridge
On their way to scattered homes.
The darkness bears no grudge
Because the people have tasted the god
Who permits himself to be eaten
By the faithful, the militant, the mindless
And the god-forsaken
About whom the god is not mistaken.
The more he is devoured, the more he lives.
He has an appetite for appetite.
He swallows those who eat him

---

* Introduction to *Breathing Spaces*, Bloodaxe 1992, p.11.

And inspires them to eat.
How sweet is the god's flesh, how sweet!
The bridge bears the weight of the shuffling feet
And no one bothers to wonder
At the black passion of water
Spelling out its own hunger
Under the bridge, under the mill
With all its small windows
Closed like books everyone has read
And nobody knows.
And the river articulates its hunger
As it bends with the creek
Twisting like need
Over mud, sedge, weed, gravel and rock.

If the god instructed the people
To enter the blackness, drink the river, eat the mud,
They would enter, drink, eat, because mud, river, blackness
Are three words of the god.
Those who eat the god
Digest the god's language
To increase their substance, deepen their shadows.
Now as they shuffle over the bridge
Their hearts beat with a deeper heartbeat,
The fields they move towards are wrapped
About their bodies like wise cloaks,
Roofs of houses are scales tipped
In their favour, the river and its creatures
Flow and thrive for the flowing people
And the eaten god is happy, finding
Himself in blood. If all is ever well

It is well now in the enlarging darkness
For the people contained as planets
In their appointed places
Each one of them so sure he seems to find delight
In not being able to see
His own or all those other faces
Sculpted from darkness by the selfsame hand
That motions the people home again

Through the familiar, invisible land
Where the long consequences spread like rain.

137 *PLAY*

Picture the old man of seventy years
Rehearsing his death several times a day.
Between rehearsals, he calls the youngsters
To his side. If, in old men, it is possible
To speak of some belief in innocence
This old man has it in his drowsy way.
When he resigns the world for a spell
He does so only when the children promise
On pain of cross their hearts and hope to die
That they will quietly play about the chair
Where he sits staring down at heaven
Somewhere in his mind adrift in sleep.
'Angels of the earth, angels of the air,
All angels love to play about a sleeping man
And when they play, holy is the watch they keep.'

138 *THE GOOD*

The good are vulnerable
As any bird in flight,
They do not think of safety,
Are blind to possible extinction
And when most vulnerable
Are most themselves.
The good are real as the sun,
Are best perceived through clouds
Of casual corruption
That cannot kill the luminous sufficiency
That shines on city, sea and wilderness,
Fastidiously revealing
One man to another,
Who yet will not accept
Responsibilities of light.

The good incline to praise,
To have the knack of seeing that
The best is not destroyed
Although forever threatened.
The good go naked in all weathers,
And by their nakedness rebuke
The small protective sanities
That hide men from themselves.
The good are difficult to see
Though open, rare, destructible;
Always, they retain a kind of youth,
The vulnerable grace
Of any bird in flight,
Content to be itself,
Accomplished master and potential victim,
Accepting what the earth or sky intends.
I think that I know one or two
Among my friends.

139 *HOUSE*

I am youth slipping like water
From that cracked tap in the yard.
They are many. I am one.
Thinking of me, they will always be children.
Every leaving will be a return
To me who sheltered their dead.
They ran to me out of streets and fields
When I gave them the smell of hot bread.
That oven in my belly
Helped them grow in the sun.
They are many. I am one.
They will live in others,
Stare out of cities, over seas
To find me,
They will hear their noisy hearts
Beat in my silence,
They will not overcome the surprise
Of finding surprise in me,

They will scour a world for evidence
Of what never dies in me.

They happened in me.
They can happen only once.
This drives my children out-of-sense.

Listen! You can hear the dance
Starting on the kitchen floor.
They are learning the steps
Becoming the music
Reaching the skill, the fever,
Doing what I've always wanted.
Dancing through me, dancing their beginning,
They are learning to be haunted.

140 *THE SECOND TREE*

My head sore with nightmare —
The seagulls tore the crows to death
Dipped the ripped bodies in the sewers
Of the trembling city
Dropped the shite-cake corpses on my head
Till I was buried, breathing, in a heap
Of bleeding flesh of crows, their features
Fixing in my skin like hateful glances
Thrown like knives across a room
Which for someone must be home
Where he can slip the world off like an overcoat —

I walked, stiffnecked with nightmare,
Under a sky split open like my mind
Out into the small garden at the back of the house.
I closed my eyes, breathing the morning air,
Breathing the innocent air.
I opened my eyes and saw a pear on the ground
Nearly hidden in the grass.
I picked it up and felt its coolness
Thrill my fingers, then my blood, my being.

I tasted it. And I knew,
As though I were another Adam
To whom another tree, a second tree
In some small corner growing unseen,
Were shown by accident
At the moment of his deepest need,
What nightmare hungered for
As it regrouped its battering legions
Of packed, implacable assassins
To savage vulnerable sleep,
The cool, moist taste, caressed by grass,
Of sanity, clear, sweet, miraculously
Normal, so near it must always be easily
Lost.
                              I could have knelt
Before the second tree, but stood in silence
While my mind rejoiced in priceless quiet
Then turned towards a human voice,
Eating the garden's flesh as I entered the house, dumb with gratitude.

NUALA NÍ DHOMHNAILL (b.1952)

Nuala Ní Dhomhnaill was born in Lancashire (England) but grew up in an Irish speaking area (Gaeltacht) in Kerry in the west of Ireland. She now lives in Dublin with her Turkish husband and four children. She writes as a woman, from her own experience, weaving Ireland's past and present, the mythological and mundane, Christian and pagan, into a rich and evocative tapestry.

141 *PARTHENOGENESIS*

Once, a lady of the Ó Moores
(married seven years without a child)
swam in the sea in summertime.
She swam well, and the day
was fine as Ireland ever saw
not even a puff of wind in the air
all the day calm, all the sea smooth —
a sheet of glass — supple, she struck out
with strength for the breaking waves
and frisked, elated by the world.
She ducked beneath the surface and there saw
what seemed a shadow, like a man's
And every twist and turn she made
the shadow did the same
and came close enough to touch.
Heart jumped and sound stopped in her mouth
her pulses ran and raced, sides near burst
The lower currents with their ice
pierced her to the bone
and the noise of the abyss numbed all her limbs
then scales grew on her skin . . .

the lure of the quiet dreamy undersea . . .
desire to escape to sea and shells . . .
the seaweed tresses where at last
her bones changed into coral
and time made atolls of her arms,
pearls of her eyes in deep long sleep,
at rest in a nest of weed,
secure as feather beds . . .
But stop!
Her heroic heritage was there,
she rose with speedy, threshing feet
and made in desperation for the beach:
with nimble supple strokes she made the sand.

Near death until the day,
some nine months later
she gave birth to a boy.
She and her husband so satisfied,
so full of love for this new son
forgot the shadow in the sea

and did not see what only the midwife saw —
stalks of sea-tangle in the boy's hair
small shellfish and sea-ribbons
and his two big eyes
as blue and limpid as lagoons.
A poor scholar passing by
who found lodging for the night
saw the boy's eyes never closed
in dark or light and when all the world slept
he asked the boy beside the fire
'Who are your people?' Came the prompt reply
'Sea People.'

This same tale is told in the West
but the woman's an Ó Flaherty
and tis the same in the South
where the lady's called Ó Shea:
this tale is told on every coast.
But whoever she was I want to say

that the fear she felt
when the sea-shadow followed her
is the same fear that vexed
the young heart of the Virgin
when she heard the angel's sweet bell
and in her womb was made flesh
by all accounts
the Son of the Living God.

142 *ABDUCTION*

The fairy woman walked
into my poem.
She closed no door
She asked no by-your-leave.
Knowing my place
I did not tell her go.
I played the woman-of-no-welcomes trick
and said:

'What's your hurry, here's your hat.
Pull up to the fire,
eat and drink what you get —
but if I were in your house
as you are in my house
I'd go home straight away
but anyway, stay.'

She stayed. Got up and pottered
round the house. Dressed the beds
washed the ware. Put the dirty clothes
in the washing-machine.
When my husband came home for his tea
he didn't know what he had wasn't me.

For I am in the fairy field
in lasting darkness
and frozen with the cold there
dressed only in white mist.

And if he wants me back
there is a solution —
get the sock of a plough
smear it with butter
and redden it with fire.

And then let him to go the bed
where lies the succubus
and press her with red iron.
'Push in into her face,
burn and brand her,

and as she fades before your eyes
I'll materialise
and as she fades before your eyes
I'll materialise.'

143 *CHRISTMAS DINNER*

The Christmas meal is over.
We were quick to knock it back.
We lapped up celery soup with zest
turkey, bacon, pies and now, mince tarts.
Our bellies full, our bones around the table.
The Christmas candle throws its little light
and the scarlet holly berries glow.

I count those present. We're all there
(seldom now together in one place.)
The fledglings are long scattered
making their own nests — we are the old clutch.
You'd swear you were caged with the tropical birds
in the Zoo with the chirping and fluttering
some mouthing, the rest up to the gunnells
with drink and jollity, with noise and crack.

Suddenly there's silence. An angel passes over
the roof. In the quietness — a sudden sneeze.
We call God's blessing on our house.
Someone farts. We laugh and say

'Better down than up!'
We're well used to the old saws
(though they have nothing to do with our lives
They come readily to our lips).

My brother stands up, goes to the door.
But there's no one there, out in the dark
not a soul, not a sinner, no Christian being.
'Dhera, an arrow struck your ear — the fairies
I'm sure are walking the hill.
You'd better come in and close the door
for fear we'll get a puck.'

Said the trickster in our midst and I hear in the babble
someone speak of 'St. Michael the Archangel
our protection in time of battle' and how
this prayer ends all fear of the dead
fear of demons of the air and all evil things.
I raise my eyes and outside the magic circle
I see Loki, a bow of mistletoe in his hand,

He offers it beguilingly to the blind old man
waffling away from the shelter
of the oak tree. Listen, tis not your ear
the next arrow will strike, Baldor, beloved brother.

144 *ISLAND*

Your body an island
in the great ocean.
Your limbs spread
on a bright sheet
over a sea of gulls.

Your forehead a spring well
mix of blood and honey —
it gave me a cooling drink
when I was burning
a healing drink
when I was feverish.

Your eyes
are mountain lakes
a lovely August day
when the sky
sparkles in the waters.
Flowing reeds your eyelashes
growing at their margins

And if I had a boat
to go to you
a white bronze boat
not a feather out of place on it
but one feather
red feather with white back
making music
to my self on board

I'd put up
the soft white billowing sails: I'd plough
through high seas
and I would come
where you lie
solitary, emerald,
insular.

145 *ANNUNCIATIONS*

She remembered to the very end
the angelic vision
in the temple:
the flutter of wings
about her —
noting the noise of doves,
sun-rays raining
on lime-white walls —
the day she got the tidings.

He —
he went away

and perhaps forgot
what grew from his loins —
two thousand years
of carrying a cross
two thousand years
of smoke and fire
of rows that reached a greater span
than all the spires of the Vatican.

Remember
O most tender virgin Mary
that never was it known
that a man came to you
in the darkness alone,
his feet bare, his teeth white
and roguery swelling in his eyes.

146 *MASCULUS GIGANTICUS HIBERNICUS*

Country lout, knife thrower (dagger-wielder)
whether in jeans or a devil at noon
all dolled up in your pinstriped suit
you're always after the one thing.

Dangerous relic from the Iron Age
you sit in pubs and devise
the treacherous plan
that does not recoil on you —
a vengeful incursion to female land.

Because you will not dare to halt the growth
of the dark-red damask rose in your mother's heart
you will have to turn the garden
to a trampled mess
pounded and ruined by your two broad hooves.

And you're frisky, prancing, antlered —
your bread is baked.
You'd live off the furze

or the heather that grows
on a young girl's sunny slopes.

147 *MARVELLOUS GRASS*

When you were a holy priest
in the middle of Mass in your purple robes
your linen mantle, your stole, your chasuble.
you saw my face in the crowd
approaching you for communion
and you dropped the blessed host.

I — I said nothing.
I was ashamed.
My lips were locked.
But still it lay on my heart
like a mud-thorn until
it penetrated my insides.
From it I nearly died.

Not long till I took to my bed:
medical experts came in hundreds
doctors, priests and friars —
not one could cure me
they abandoned me for death.

Go out, men:
take with you spades and scythes
sickles, hoes and shovels.
Ransack the ruins
cut the bushes, clear the rubble,
the rank growth, the dust, the misery
that grows on my tragic grassland.

And in the place where fell
the sacred host you will see
among the useless plants
a patch of marvellous grass.

Let the priest come and with his fingers
take dexterously the sacred host.
And it's given to me: on my tongue
it will melt and I will sit up in the bed
as healthy as I was when young.

148 *GREAT MOTHER*

Maiden and mother, oh nurse, oh atom bomb,
you will spurt on us the black liquid milk,
volcano dust will burst from your throat
from your heart the burnt smell be stripped.

We have avoided your gluttonous embrace:
arrogant angels, we built our tower of Babel
with the help of science: we leapt into the skies
with a hop and a skip and a gambol.

The seven-league boots of conscience can't keep up,
dwarfs in motion, spoilt brats apeing
adult behaviour — animals in disguise.
In this unruly house our acts have neither finish nor *finesse*.

The fringe of your cloak is on the horizon:
you will wrap us in *your* great-coat of clay,
we'll be extinguished with kisses, drenched with bitter tears
of acid rain — our own home-brewed rain.

149 *MONK*

You are St Anthony
or some other saint
sitting in your rocky hermitage.
You make the sign of the cross —
wind and sea no longer toss.
Your hands are full of larks.

I am Temptation.
You know me.
Sometimes I'm Eve,
sometimes the snake:
I slide into your reverie
in the middle of brightest day.
I shine like the sun in an orchard.

But it's not to torment you
every day I rise —
but to drown you
in love's delights.
I'm a dead hero leaping
from the edge of the bridge of fear —
That's the only reason I haunt you:
my monk, my apostle, my priest.

150 *MISCARRIAGE ABROAD*

You, embryo, moving in me —
I welcomed your emerging
I said I'd rear you carefully
in the manner of my new people —

under your pillow the holy book,
in your cot, bread and a needle:
your father's shirt as an eiderdown
at your head a brush for sweeping.

I was brimming
with happiness
until the dykes broke
and out was swept
a ten-weeks frog —
'the best-laid schemes . . .'

And now it's March
your birthday that never was —
and white ribbons of tide
remind me of baby-clothes,
an imbecile's tangled threads.

And I will not go to see
my best friend's new born child
because of the jealousy
that stares from my evil eye.

ANJELA DUVAL (1905-1981)

Anjela Duval was born into a long line of Breton peasant farmers, and as the only surviving child inherited the family smallholding in the Leger River valley, a farm which had passed down from one generation to another through the maternal line. After only four years of primary schooling Anjela worked full time on the land, as she continued to do until prevented by sickness in her old age. In her forties, after the death of her parents, Duval coped with depression and loneliness by reading Breton literature, which gave her a new goal in life — the nationalist struggle and defence of the Breton language. Her first poems were published in the 1960s, and with the resurgence of Breton nationalism in the 1970s they brought her considerable notoriety. Her poetry deals with her attachment to the land and her life as a farmer, her love of trees and of the natural world, the Roman Catholic faith in which she was raised, and the human community, be it her deceased loved ones or the Breton nation as a whole.

151 *SAINT MARY*

Saint Mary, Mother of God,
Preserve for me a child's heart,
Pure and transparent as a spring,
A heart simple and straight,
That will never taste unhappiness.
A devoted heart,
Tender and grateful,
A heart loyal and generous,
That will not forget goodness,
And will not hold on to evil.
Make for me a humble and patient heart,

*This information is from Lenora A. Timm's Introduction to *A Modern Breton Political Poet, Anjela Duval: A Biography and An Anthology*, Edwin Mellen Press 1990.

Loving without expecting a return.
Content to leave in a beloved heart
The first place for your Son.
A lofty and invincible heart,
That no ignorance will be able to close,
That no insensitivity will be able to expend.
A heart wrought with the glory of Christ,
Pierced with His love,
Whose wound would not heal
Except in heaven.

152 *A MARVELOUS HOUR*

The day is now over.
The hour's come I was waiting for.
After labour so material,
How sweet a spiritual hour.

I'm bathed here in tranquillity.
I hear no sound around me.
But the sound of the pendulum,
Counting out the drops of time.

The hour of prayer, hour of study.
Hour of dreaming, of fantasy,
Hour divine, full of ecstasy.

In this hour there's so much happiness!
Only one thing's missing to perfect it:
— In the hearth the singing of a cricket! . . .

153 *MELANCHOLY*

I am gathering ferns,
The nicest of jobs, you might say . . .
True, but it's hot,
Let's stop for a moment.

. . .

On my arm a sickle and a pitchfork,
in my hand a fern
fine and light like a piece of lace
on the edge of the field I sit down
In the shade of the chestnut tree.

. . .

A sharp perfume, a dizzying perfume
the ferns turning
while tickling my nostrils
have gone to my head.
And here I am beginning to daydream,
my mind wandering
down the path of memories;
where before me passes
as on a brilliant screen
my bygone youth.

And I think of the past
that will never return!
The autumn of my life,
Ah, golden-brown fern,
symbol of arid and poor soil,
such a fate is ours!
Sterile. Unimportant. Meaningless.
I would at least wish to be like you,
also able to produce a perfume:
a sharp, dizzying perfume
of pure poetry.

154 *LINDENS*

Thirteen linden trees stand thick together
One against the other on a dry bank
Their heads held straight in the blue heaven
At a time when I was young
They were already grown
Thirteen lindens in a cluster

A bouquet of dark green
Immense. Giants
On the horizon.

These lindens are not my possession
Yet I possess the right
To cut them down.
They are sucking the sap of my land
With their roots so long. But I won't.
I would miss them.
They are my organ,
They are my harp,
When the wind plays on them
Its thousand different notes.
When the crow caws
On their bare winter branches
When on their dark summits
The yellow-beaked blackbird whistles,
And when from their highest limb flow
The crystal drops
Of the nightingale.

155 *MY HEART*

My heart is a Cemetery
In it are countless graves
In it always a new grave
Graves of friends and relatives
My heart is a Cemetery!

My heart is a Cemetery
But no!
My heart is a Sanctuary
Wherein live My Dear Departed!

156 DAWN-SONG ✓

Would your soft cooing
Each morning in the chestnut tree
Be for me, russet dove?

No! I'd be crazy to think so!
Your song is a hymn
To the One who gave you
That nostalgic voice.

Your soft cooing
Is a dawn-song to your loving mate
And to your baby birds
And to all your winged friends.

. . . Who would sing for me?
An old woman without a relative or a mate!
Yet my heart is brimming with songs
For I love every Creature.

157 WORK OF THE FOREIGNER

Strip. Despoil our Country
Sweep away the sacred oaks of the Druids
The birches of the Celts and the yew-trees
— And the chestnuts of our youth —
In which our birds sang.
Start fires in the moor
In the heath. In the broom waving
Like seas of golden water
And write on the bare back
Of the old Country, in every foreign language
Poems of mourning
Ugly poems.
With their stiff letters
Rigid as their steel faces:
Long rows of lead soldiers

Tedious songs of their resin trees
With strange names!
And soon . . . if we don't pay attention
On the great organ
Of their dark and sad forests
— Fertilised with the ashes of our trees —
The Atlantic Wind
Will play while singing
        . . . The Requiem of our Country.

158 *MISUNDERSTANDING*

What's in it for you to stir up
My too tender heart?
Why do you inflame
My too active brain with madness?
You know very well
— or don't you know? —
— In spite of an invincible love —
There are too many differences between us
Between city-dwellers and peasants.

Their mockery has wounded me
And my audacity has wounded them
— Why that misunderstanding
Eternally between us?
— Why mock us
Scorn us
Make fun of us
Although we love you
The sap of your living heart
Of your bare earth — of my Country!
My Brittany. My love. My Life.
They love you too — they say —
— Yes then! Your brilliant multicoloured skirt
Your green woods. Your streams.
Your golden heath. Your alluring seas.
Your birds and your flowers.

But they should be repulsed
To hold between their white fingers
A handful of Soil of their Country
Soaked so often with the sweat
        — and blood —
Of generations of Bretons.

Because of love for you
Sacred Soil of my Country
We suffer that disrespect
        — done to you —
To be despised for loving you too much
Brittany, my only love
For you all my strength until the last spark
Until the hour when you will open my arms
On my rageless and lifeless body
While my ardent Soul passes
Toward the Paradise of our Race.

159 *IN THE FOREST*

On the soft carpet of the forest
To go on velvet footsteps
To sit at your feet
In the dappled sunlight, in silence
Far from the sounds of humans
To listen to the rustling of your leaves . . .
And to caress alternatively
With my hand and my look . . .
In a soft voice I call you
Using your magical names:
White-oak. Forest-aspen.
Maple. Hornbeam.
Black-alder. Willow. White Birch.

My thousand mute friends.

160 *YOUR PAIN IS YOURS*

You may share
With one you care for
    Your goods
    Your knowledge
    Your love
    Your happiness
There's one thing you won't share:
    Your pain
    For that's been cut
To just your measure.

161 *WHY?*

They are heedless
Those who walk on city pavements.
Heedless of killing and injuring
Small creatures moving or not . . .
Ah. How heedful I am at each step
Heedful of crushing, of smashing
Along the path or through the field
Tiny humble creatures beneath my foot:
The green beetle crouched in the moss,
The minute ant carrying
With great effort and ingenuity
The short-straw to her anthill.
Pretty little flowers half-hidden in the grass,
Trying to open their heart to the Sun.
It seems to me that I hear their lament:
— Why then, Lord, did you not give
Wings to man?
Ah! How heavy is the weight of his foot on us!

162 *A CHILD'S FEELING*

Such love as that for the trees?
From my tenderest age
When I caressed their bark
With my babyish hand.
When I glued my ear against them
To listen to the rustling of their leaves
The humming of their branches twisting in a high wind.
And the snap of their dry twigs breaking off.
          When I tried to climb high, high!
Ever higher. From limb to limb.
          A bird without wings!
And from there to marvel at the horizon.

. . . And how unpleasant the descent
To touch one's feet on the ground!

Trees of my childhood, tell me then
Where it came from so early
A love so profound for you?

Perhaps I was a tree
                    at the beginning of time . . .

163 *PRAYER FOR A NEW YEAR*

Lord! Father of the Universe
And Father of all Creatures
Spirit and Matter
Today hear if she asks
The least of your children
Who loves you from the depths of her heart
Her happiness to live forever . . .
Before you like a child before his father
With neither pain nor suspicion
I start a new Year
In the beginning of the springtime.

What will I be? I am in your hands.
Respectful? . . . Yes. Obedient? Hardly . . .
But may Your Will be done
And may a morsel of wisdom descend on my old age
So that my time will not be empty or vain
Give me Love and Enlightenment
Sufficient to share with others who
Stumble and grope on the Way
The Way so narrow that leads to Eternity . . .

Amen.

SOURCES AND ACKNOWLEDGEMENTS

The translations in the medieval sections are by Oliver Davies, unless otherwise indicated, although in many cases we must acknowledge a debt to previous translators.

Medieval Religious Poetry

1. Text in Ifor Williams, *The Beginnings of Welsh Poetry* (Cardiff, 1972), p. 102.
2. Text in A. O. H. Jarman, ed., *Llyfr Du Caerfyrddin* (Cardiff, 1982), p. 16. Text slightly emended.
3. Gerard Murphy, *Early Irish Lyrics* (Oxford, 1956), p. 4.
4. R. I. Best, *Ériu* 4, p. 120.
5. Murphy, p. 4.
6. Jarman, pp. 17–18.
7. Jarman, p. 9.
8. Jarman, pp. 13–14.
9. Brian ó Cuív, *Ériu* 19, pp. 4–5.
10. Kuno Meyer, *Ériu* 2, pp. 55–56.
11. Kuno Meyer, *Ériu* 3, p. 14.
12. Jarman, p. 15.
13. James Carney, *Ériu* 22, pp. 27–28.
14. Kuno Meyer, *Ériu* 6, p. 112.
15. M. E. Byrne, *Ériu* 1, pp. 226–27.
16. T. P. O'Nowlan, *Ériu* 2, pp. 92–94 and Robin Flower, *Ériu* 5, p. 112.
17. Kuno Meyer, *Ériu* 6, p. 116.
18. Text in W. Stokes and J. Strachan, eds., *Thesaurus Palaeohibernicus* vol. II, (Cambridge, 1903), pp. 354–58.
19. Marged Haycock, *Blodeugerdd Barddas o Ganu Crefyddol Cynnar* (Llandybie, 1994), pp. 23–29.
20. Stokes and Strachan, p. 294.

21. Charles Plummer, ed., *Irish Litanies* (Henry Bradshaw Society, vol. LXII, London, 1925), p. 6.
22. Stokes and Strachan, p. 322.
23. G. S. M. Walker, *Sancti Columbani Opera (Scriptores Latini Hiberniae*, vol. II, Dublin, 1970), p. 214.
24. Plummer, p. 26.
25. Murphy, p. 64.
26. Haycock, pp. 165–9.
27. Henry Lewis, *Hen Gerddi Crefyddol* (Cardiff, 1931), pp. 21–22.
28. Lewis, pp. 57–59.
29. Jarman, p. 59.
30. Jarman, p. 54 (text slightly emended).
31. Thomas Parry, ed., *Gwaith Dafydd ap Gwilym* (Cardiff, 1952).
32. Haycock, pp. 30–40.
33. E. Ernaut, ed., *Le Mirouer de la Mort* (Paris, 1914), p. 62.
34. Thomas Parry, ed., *The Oxford Book of Welsh Verse* (Oxford, 1962), pp. 332–39.
35. Brendan O'Malley, ed., *A Welsh Pilgrim's Manual* (Llandysul, 1989), pp. 32–36 (translated by Cynthia Davies). Our thanks to Gomer Press and to the editor of the volume, the Reverend Brendan O'Malley, for permission to reprint these translations.

Medieval Religious Prose

36. *Patrologia Latina* 40, 1031–46.
37. *Patrologia Latina Supplementum* I, 1375–80.
38. *Corpus Scriptorum Ecclesiasticorum Latinorum* 29, 436–59.
39. *Patrologia Latina* 72, 775–90.
40. *Archaeologia Cambrensis* (1894), 139–42.
41. Stanley Miller Dahlmann, *Critical Edition of the Buched Beuno*, PhD, Catholic University of America, Washington, 1976.
42. J. W. James, *Rhigyfarch's Life of St David*, Cardiff, 1967.
43. J. Pinkerton, *Vitae antiquae sanctorum . . . in Scotia* (London, 1789), pp. 1–23.
44. Ludwig Bieler, *The Irish Penitentials* (Dublin, 1963), pp. 108–10, 133–35. I acknowledge a debt to Bieler for my own translation.
45. Walker, pp. 72–74.
46. Walker, pp. 116–20.
47. J. Strachan, *Ériu* 3, pp. 1–10.

48. W. Stokes, *Ériu* 2, pp. 96–162.
49. E. J. Gwynn, *Ériu* 2, pp. 82–83.
50. P. J. Donovan, ed., *Ysgrifeniadau Byrion Morgan Llwyd* (Cardiff, 1985), pp. 1–3.
51. Eifion Evans, *Daniel Rowland and the Great Evangelical Awakening in Wales* (Banner of Truth Trust, 1985), pp. 51ff.

The Carmina Gadelica

The following numbers refer to the volume and item numbers of the individual pieces as printed in the 1928 edition of the first two volumes of the *Carmina Gadelica*, and the 1940 edition of Volume III, all published by Scottish Academic Press in Edinburgh. In these editions the Gaelic and English are on facing pages and the numbering is consecutive, from 1 to 351 over the three volumes. Volumes I and II were originally published in 1900 and were edited and translated by Alexander Carmichael. Volume III was edited from Carmichael's notes by his grandson, Professor James Carmichael Watson (see Appendix).

52. I, 1
53. I, 2
54. I, 3
55. I, 14
56. I, 18
57. I, 19
58. I, 20
59. I, 26
60. I, 33
61. I, 38
62. I, 43
63. I, 50
64. I, 51
65. I, 52
66. I, 54
67. II, 194
68. II, 203
69. II, 206
70. I, 70
71. I, 71
72. I, 73

SOURCES AND ACKNOWLEDGEMENTS

73. I, 74
74. I, 76
75. I, 77
76. I, 82
77. I, 84
78. I, 92
79. I, 93
80. I, 114
81. I, 116
82. I, 118
83. I, 121
84. III, 225
85. III, 231
86. III, 232
87. III, 242
88. III, 248
89. III, 249
90. III, 272
91. III, 277
92. III, 316
93. III, 321
94. III, 327
95. III, 328
96. III, 331
97. III, 343
98. III, 350

The Religious Songs of Connacht

The following numbers refer to the volumes of *The Religious Songs of Connacht*. Volume I comprises Chapter 6 and Volume II Chapter 7 of a longer work, *The Songs of Connacht*, all edited and in the case of oral pieces translated by Douglas Hyde. The extracts in this work are from the 1972 Irish University Press edition which reproduces the original 1906 volumes in a single cover, with an Introduction by Dominic Daly.

99–103. Volume I
104–111. Volume II

236

Modern Poetry

112. Translation by Oliver Davies. Welsh original, '*Difiau Dyrchafael*' is reprinted in Medwin Hughes, ed., *Blodeugerdd Barddas O Gerddi Crefyddol* (Barddas, 1993).

113. Translation by Oliver Davies. Welsh original, '*Y Griafolen*' is reprinted in *Euros Bowen, Priest-Poet/Bardd-Offeiriad*, edited by Cynthia and Saunders Davies (Church in Wales Publications, 1993). All the poems by Euros Bowen were written in Welsh.

114. Translation Euros Bowen, ibid. We acknowledge with thanks permission granted by the Board of Mission of the Church in Wales to reproduce this and the following poems by Euros Bowen (nos. 114–120) from *Priest-Poet/Bardd-Offeiriad*.

115. Translation Euros Bowen.

116–120. Translation Cynthia Davies.

121. From *The Wreck of the Archangel*, John Murray (London, 1989). Reproduced with permission of the publisher, acknowledged with thanks.

122–133. From *Selected Poems* (Seren Poetry Wales Press, 1992). Reproduced with kind permission of the author, Ruth Bidgood, and Seren.

134. From W. R. Rogers, *Poems* (The Gallery Press, 1971). By kind permission of the author and The Gallery Press.

135. From Gladys Mary Coles, *The Glass Island* (Duckworth, 1992) by kind permission of the author and Duckworth.

136–140. From Brendan Kennelly, *Breathing Spaces: Early Poems*, (Bloodaxe Books, 1992). Reprinted by permission of Bloodaxe Books Ltd.

141–150. From Nuala Ní Dhomhnaill, *Selected Poems: Rogha Dánta*, translated by Michael Hartnett (The Raven Arts Press, Dublin, 1992). Reprinted by kind permission of the author and New Island Books.

151–163. The poems by Duval were all written in Breton and translated into English by Lenora A. Timm. We are grateful to both Lenora Timm and Edwin Mellen Press for permission to reproduce them here.

APPENDIX: EDITIONS OF THE
CARMINA GADELICA

The presence of many anthologized selections from the *Carmina Gadelica*, and its widespread popularity in recent years, have given Carmichael's collection of Gaelic oral literature a notoriety unusual in the field of Victorian folklore. The following notes may be of use to readers who wish to orientate themselves with respect to the original publication of these volumes.

Alexander Carmichael published the first two volumes in 1900, being the result of some fifty years of recording the religious oral literature and folklore of the Gaelic speakers of the Highlands and Islands of Scotland. It came out under the Gaelic and Latin title *Ortha Nan Gaidheal/Carmina Gadelica*: *Hymns and Incantations*, with the subtitle, 'With Illustrative Notes on Words, Rites, and Customs, Dying and Obsolete: Orally Collected in the Highlands and Islands of Scotland and Translated into English by Alexander Carmichael' (published by T. & A. Constable, Edinburgh). Before his death Carmichael also started to prepare material for a third volume, which was finally edited and published by his grandson, Professor James Carmichael Watson in 1940, followed by Volume IV in 1941 (both published by Oliver & Boyd, Edinburgh). The first two volumes were reprinted by Oliver and Boyd in 1928 with minor corrections by Carmichael's daughter, Ella, a reputed Gaelic scholar in her own right. Scottish Academic Press brought out further bilingual editions in 1983/4.

Two further volumes based on Carmichael's original unpublished manuscripts were edited by Angus Matheson. Volume V consists mainly of secular poetry (Oliver & Boyd, Edinburgh, 1954) and Volume VI contains indexes and bibliographical information (Scottish Academic Press, 1971). All six volumes retain the bilingual format, with the Gaelic on the left-hand folio and the English translation facing it. Illustrative notes are in English, but with extensive Gaelic quotations.

In 1992 Floris Books (Edinburgh) produced an English paperback version of the *Carmina Gadelica* in a single volume. Most of Carmichael's notes and comments are retained but are placed at the end rather than with the passages to which they refer, and do not follow the numbering of earlier editions. In addition to these full-length versions of the *Carmina Gadelica* there are numerous English selections, usually concentrating on the more immediately accessible and less obviously 'pagan' elements of the original. While they bring the material to a wide readership a reading of the work in its entirety is to be recommended to anyone wishing to make a balanced assessment of Carmichael's extensive original collection. It is also worth pointing out, lest the nineteenth-century Highlanders be seen as excessively pious, that the religious material was only one genre of oral literature. As with Hyde's *Songs of Connacht*, Carmichael might well have included love songs, drinking songs, tales of heroic battles and of inter-clan rivalries had these been his interests.

SELECT BIBLIOGRAPHY

(For texts included in this anthology, see the references given in
Sources and Acknowledgements)

General

Allchin, A. M., *Praise above All: Discovering the Welsh Tradition*, Cardiff,
1991.

Bradley, Ian, *The Celtic Way*, London, 1993.

Davies, Oliver, *Celtic Christianity in Early Medieval Wales*, Cardiff, 1995
(forthcoming).

Davies, Oliver, *Celtic Spirituality*, Classics of Western Spirituality, New
York (forthcoming).

Davies, Wendy, 'The Myth of the Celtic Church' in Nancy Edwards
and Alan Lane, eds., *The Early Church in Wales and the West*, Oxbow,
1992, 12–21.

De Waal, Esther, *A World Made Whole*, London, 1992.

Flower, Robin, *The Irish Tradition*, Oxford, 1947.

Hughes, Kathleen, 'The Celtic Church: is this a Valid Concept?' in
Cambridge Medieval Celtic Studies, 1 (1981), 1–20.

Kenny, J. F., *The Sources for the Early History of Ireland*, Dublin, 1929.

Lapidge, M. and Sharpe, R., *A Bibliography of Celtic-Latin Literature
400-1200*, Dublin, 1985.

Mackey, J. P., ed., *An Introduction to Celtic Christianity*, Edinburgh, 1989.

Maher, Michael, ed., *Irish Spirituality*, Dublin, 1981.

O'Donoghue, Noel Dermot, *The Mountain Beyond the Mountain*, Edinburgh, 1993.

Piggot, Stuart, *Ancient Britons and the Antiquarian Imagination*, Thames
and Hudson, 1989.

Sims-Williams, Patrick, 'The Visionary Celt: the Construction of an
Ethnic Preconception' in *Cambridge Medieval Celtic Studies*, 11
(1986), 71–96.

Sims-Williams, Patrick, 'Some Celtic Otherworld Terms' in *Celtic Language, Celtic Culture: a Festschrift for Eric P. Hamp*, California, 1990, 6–81.

Thomas, Patrick, *Candle in the Darkness*, Llandysul, 1993.

Pre-Christian Celtic Religion

Brunaux, Jean Louis, *The Celtic Gauls: Gods, Rites and Sanctuaries*, London, 1988 (English translation).

Chadwick, Nora, *The Celts*, London, 1971.

Condran, Mary, *The Serpent and the Goddess*, San Francisco, 1989.

Cunliffe, Barry, *The Celtic World*, London, 1992.

Green, Miranda, *The Gods of the Celts*, Stroud, 1986.

Green, Miranda, *Symbol and Image in Celtic Religious Art*, London, 1989.

Hutton, Ronald, *The Pagan Religions of the Ancient British Isles*, London, 1991.

Piggot, Stuart, *The Druids*, London, 1968.

Wait, G.A., *Ritual and Religion in Iron Age Britain*, British Archaeological Reports, British Series, 149, 1985.

Webster, Graham, *The British Celts and their Gods under Rome*, London, 1986.

Church History and Archaeology

Bieler, Ludwig, *The Irish Penitentials*, Dublin, 1963.

Chadwick, Nora, *Early Brittany*, Cardiff, 1969.

N. Chadwick, K. Hughes, C. Brooke, K. Jackson, eds., *Studies in the British Church*, Cambridge, 1958.

Cowley, F. G., *A History of the Monastic Order in South Wales*, Cardiff, 1977.

Davies, Wendy, *Wales in the Early Middle Ages*, Leicester, 1982, 141–93.

de Paor, Liam, *St Patrick's World*, Co. Dublin, 1993.

Edwards, Nancy and Lane, Alan, eds., *The Early Church in Wales and the West*, Oxbow, 1992.

Hughes, Kathleen, *The Church in Early Irish Society*, London, 1966.

Hughes, Kathleen, *Early Christian Ireland: Introduction to the Sources*, London, 1972.

Pryce, Huw, 'Pastoral Care in Early Medieval Wales' in John Blair and Richard Sharpe, eds., *Pastoral Care before the Parish*, Leicester, 1991, 41–62.

Pryce, Huw, *Native Law and the Church in Medieval Wales*, Oxford, 1993.

Richter, Michael, *The Enduring Tradition*, London, 1988.

Thomas, Charles, *Christianity in Roman Britain to AD 500*, London, 1981.

Thompson, E. A., *Saint Germanus of Auxerre and the End of Roman Britain*, Woodbridge, 1984.

Walsh, J. and Bradley, T., *A History of the Irish Church 400-700 AD*, Co. Dublin, 1991.

Williams, David, *The Welsh Cistercians*, Tenby, 1984.

Williams, Glanmor, 'Some Protestant Views of Early British Church History' in *Welsh Reformation Essays*, Cardiff, 1967, 207-19.

Williams, Glanmor, *The Welsh Church from Conquest to Reformation*, Cardiff, 1976.

Williams, Glanmor, *The Welsh and their Religion*, Cardiff, 1991.

Hagiography

Baring-Gould, S. and Fisher, J., eds., *The Lives of the British Saints*, I-IV, London, 1907–1913.

Bowen, E. G., *Saints, Seaways and Settlements*, Cardiff, 1969.

Evans, D. Simon, *The Welsh Life of David*, Cardiff, 1988 (English translation).

Hawley, John Stratton, *Saints and Virtues*, California, 1987.

Heffernan, Thomas J., *Sacred Biography*, New York and Oxford, 1988.

Henken, Elissa R., *Traditions of the Welsh Saints*, Woodbridge, 1987.

Henken, Ellisa R., *The Welsh Saints: a Study in Patterned Lives*, Woodbridge, 1991.

James, J. W., *Rhigyfarch's Life of Saint David*, Cardiff, 1967.

Jones, Francis, *The Holy Wells of Wales*, Cardiff, 1954.

Kieckhefer, Richard, 'Imitators of Christ: Sainthood in the Christian Tradition' in Richard Kieckhefer and George D. Bond, eds., *Sainthood: its Manifestations in World Religions*, California, 1988.

O'Donoghue, Noel Dermot, *Aristocracy of Soul: St Patrick of Ireland*, Minnesota, 1988.

Plummer, Charles, *Vitae Sanctorum Hiberniae*, vols. I and II, Oxford, 1910.

Religious Poetry and Prose

Bloomfield, Morton W. and Dunn, Charles W., *The Role of the Poet in Early Societies*, Cambridge, 1989.

Evans, D. Simon, *Medieval Religious Literature*, Cardiff, 1986.

Haycock, Marged, *Blodeugerdd Barddas o Ganu Crefyddol Cynnar*, Llandybie, 1994.

McKenna, Catherine A., *The Medieval Welsh Religious Lyric*, Belmont, Mass., 1991.

Murphy, Gerard, ed., *Early Irish Lyrics*, Oxford, 1956.

Williams, J. E. Caerwyn, *The Irish Literary Tradition*, Cardiff and Belmont, Mass., 1992.

Art, Music and Liturgy

Edwards, Owain Tudor, *Matins, Lauds and Vespers for St David's Day*, Cambridge, 1990.

Henderson, George, *From Durrow to Kells*, London, 1987.

Henry, Francoise, *Irish Art in the Early Christian Period to A.D. 800*, London, 1965.

Travis, James, *Miscellanea Musica Celtica*, Wissenschaftliche Abhandlungen Bd. XIV, New York, 1968.

Warren, F. E., *Liturgy and Ritual of the Celtic Church* (2nd edition), Woodbridge, 1987.

Theology

Davies, Oliver, 'On Divine Love from *Food for the Soul*: a Celtic Mystical Paradigm?' in *Mystics Quarterly*, vol. XX, no. 3 (1994), 87–95.

Dumville, David, 'Late Seventh or Eighth Century Evidence for the British Transmission of Pelagius' in *Cambridge Medieval Celtic Studies*, 10 (1985), 39–52.

Evans, R. F., *Four Letters of Pelagius*, London, 1968.

Forthomme Nicholson, M., 'Celtic Theology: Pelagius' in Mackey, J. P., ed., *An Introduction to Celtic Christianity*, Edinburgh, 1989, 386–413.

Herbert, M. and McNamara, M., *Irish Biblical Apocrypha*, Edinburgh, 1989.

Moran, Dermot, *The Philosophy of John Scottus Eriugena*, Cambridge, 1989.

Rees, B. R., *Pelagius: a Reluctant Heretic*, Woodbridge, 1988.

Rees, B. R., *The Letters of Pelagius and his Followers*, Woodbridge, 1991.